YOU CAN INVEST LIKE A
STOCK MARKET PRO

HOW TO USE SIMPLE AND POWERFUL STRATEGIES OF
THE WORLD'S GREATEST INVESTORS TO BUILD WEALTH

JAMES PATTERSENN JR.

Publisher's Cataloging-in-Publication Data

Title: You can invest like a stock market pro: How to use simple and powerful strategies of the world's greatest investors to build wealth / James Pattersenn, Jr.

Description: Lancaster, SC: Trilogy Publishing Group, 2018. | Includes 23 tables and index.

Identifiers: LCCN 2017918792 | ISBN 9780989546416 (softcover) | ISBN 9780989546409 (ebook)

Subjects: LCSH: Investments—United States. | Stocks—United States. | Investment analysis. | BISAC: BUSINESS & ECONOMICS / Investments & Securities / Analysis & Trading Strategies.

Classification: LCC HG4521.P38 Y68 2018 (print) | LCC HG4521.P38 (ebook) | DDC 332.6--dc23

LC record available at https://lccn.loc.gov/2017918792

Contents

A Letter from the Author

It originally was my intention to release this book to the public in July 2014, but I had a change of mind. Here's why: As of March 29, 2014, my Personal Worry-Free Stock Portfolio had achieved an impressive annual rate of return of 24.4% and a total return of 187.5% since its inception on Sept. 15, 2008. · The return figures for the portfolio do not include dividends that were received. The S&P 500 had an annual rate of return of 9.7% and a total return of 67.1% during the same period, not including dividends. Some investment professionals felt that the returns were an exaggeration, but they were not. Others believed that the returns were legitimate but were probably the result of leverage, market timing or luck. I don't have the slightest idea of how to time the stock market, I don't believe in luck and the use of leverage is out of the question since I had previously experimented with its use and lost most of my money. Still, others thought the amazing results were the product of some great bull market run in 2008 and 2009. My newest portfolio, a *Worry-Free Traditional IRA*, also had achieved an impressive annual rate of return of 30.9% and a total return of 63.9% since its inception with dividends reinvested with the portfolio only one year and 10 months old. With that newest portfolio, I'd be the first to admit that more time was needed to establish credibility that its performance is the result of my use of the principles and strategies set forth in this book. The S&P 500 had an annual rate of return of 22.9% and a total return of 46.3% during the same period with dividends reinvested.

As I mentioned earlier, it was my intention to publish this book in July 2014. So, I began the process of sending out review copies to various review publications and investment professionals to gather their glowing comments and opinions, but I had failed to realize I had put the cart before the horse. What I should have done was consult with other investment professionals before going to print. I have since learned that any author who fails to get input from other professionals in his field before publishing his work is making a serious mistake. One individual in particular who had a significant impact on my decision to forgo publishing my book in 2014 was Mr. Douglas Pedersen, an investment pro and investment blogger (and I'm certain that he holds several more distinguished titles).

Although my intentions were good, Mr. Pedersen opened my eyes to the fact that the book was lacking in several crucial areas and failed to answer many questions. He also said I needed to turn in impressive returns for another five years in order to establish a fairly credible track record. But the most important advice I received from Mr. Pedersen was to give it more time to see how the strategies would hold up over the long term, and I have done just that. To that end, I now provide you with what I think is a much-improved version of this book.

Mr. Pedersen told me exactly what I didn't want to hear, but I realized he was 100% correct in his assessment. The way I saw it, I could either just give up on my desire to publish my book or I could act on the constructive information that I had received. As you see, I chose to do the latter.

Thank you, Mr. Pedersen. To you, I'm forever grateful.

Sincerely,

James Pattersenn Jr.

James Pattersenn Jr.

PART ONE

STOP MAKING EXCUSES — LET'S GET STARTED

INTRODUCTION

How would you like to become much wealthier than you ever thought was possible and do so without having to put forth a lot of effort? You simply buy excellent stocks, sit back, and allow the power of compounding to work its magic. I believe the individual investor can consistently churn out market-beating returns with the right investment plan or program. Many investors have amassed great fortunes from investing in stocks and the majority are men and women of average intelligence. In a March 2013 article published in *USA Today*, author Al Neuharth stated, "Most of us hope to get richer as life goes on. All of us should realize that the surest way to do that is by smart and regular investments in the stock market." So, it is very possible for persons of average intelligence to build wealth from investing in individual stocks or the stock market. In addition to building wealth, a good investment program or plan should result in little to no worry for the investor. A good investment program is usually a boring one that allows an investor to sleep well at night — and most investment pros I have studied proudly claim to sleep very well at night.

I have spent many years researching the best and most effective strategies and principles for becoming wealthy by investing in stocks while minimizing risk as much as possible, and this book is my attempt to share the knowledge I have gained with you. By doing so, it is my hope you will be worry-free in your investment choices and will have confidence the investments you select have proven themselves to be wealth-builders, regardless of what is happening with the economy or the stock market. Within this book, you are provided some fantastic information to help you to become a better investor, including the selection process for picking great stocks, determining what to pay for them, when to sell, tools of the trade and much more. Also included are the lessons I have learned from my experiences as an investor. Most importantly,

I've given you the same principles and strategies used by some of the world's most successful stock market pros. I have made every attempt to present the information in this book in a clear, concise and understandable manner so you can begin putting it to use immediately — so you, too, can invest like a stock market pro.

"You get out of an investment what you put into it, so the first decision you have to make is how much time you are prepared to devote to the initial task of acquiring a basic knowledge of investment." —Jim Slater

YES! YOU CAN INVEST LIKE A PRO!

You may be wondering if you are capable of learning the information presented in this book. Most people think it takes great intelligence to learn how to successfully invest in stocks, but, fortunately, that isn't entirely true. If it were, I certainly wouldn't have been qualified to write this book, nor would I have achieved the amazing returns that I have. I consider myself a person of average intelligence, but I must admit I'm very pleased with the success I have enjoyed through stock investing since 2008. So, when I say, "Yes! You can invest like a stock market pro!" I really mean it. It really isn't that difficult, though it will take some time and dedication to the process.

Most successful investors will tell us to keep things simple when it comes to investing and to stay away from investment systems, principles and strategies that are too complex because they usually don't work, only work for a short time, or only make the inventors or creators that sell them very rich. The world's best pros are able to consistently obtain market-beating returns, and are able to do so over the long term. What's even more amazing is those pros are convinced the small or individual investor can do the same; in other words, these great investors believe the small or individual investor can invest like a stock market pro, just like I do. Although there are many pundits that say it is impossible to beat the market, Sir John Templeton, Peter Lynch, Jim Slater and numerous other great investors have said you and I can beat the stock market over the long term — and to me, that's what counts. Even the amazing and energetic Jim Cramer, of the very popular show *Mad Money*, believes that individual investors can beat the market by holding between five and 10 stocks in their portfolios and actively managing those positions. Yes, the intriguing Jim Cramer believes we must actively manage our stocks and not buy-and-forget them, and I fully agree. If you can consistently beat the market long term, you definitely are investing like a pro!

The principles and strategies included within this book are easy to learn and simple to use, and I can say they work without a doubt. As a matter of fact, they have worked for some of the world's best and most successful investment pros and are still working for many of them because are the ones who have created and perfected these techniques. I simply have compiled and organized their information in an easy-to-read format. Since this book contains some elements of several popular stock investment styles or strategies that exist, I simply call it "worry-free investing" to distinguish it from other systems or programs; thus, I will on numerous occasions refer to you or myself as worry-free investors, because if you are going to invest like the pros do, you have no business worrying when it comes to your portfolio.

"Twenty years in this business convinces me that any normal person using the customary 3% of the brain can pick stocks just as well, if not better, than the average Wall Street expert." —Peter Lynch

CAN YOU AFFORD NOT TO INVEST?

All too often, people fail to invest in their future because they believe they simply cannot afford to invest, don't have the time to invest, or that investing is just too difficult. This way of thinking begs a few questions: Can you afford to be old and broke? Do you want to struggle financially all of your life? Do you want to depend on someone else, yet, still barely get by? Well, my response to every question is, "I don't!"

Here in the United States, one of the richest nations in the world, it's common to see Americans still working well past their retirement age — and not because they want to, but because they must. We see the elderly working in the local grocery store or at Wal-Mart. These same people have spent their lives working and paying taxes, yet, many now have to wrestle with serious choices, such as whether to pay their electric bill instead of buying an essential medication they need to live a more productive life. I personally have visited the homes of many of the elderly, and I have a great insight into the daily financial struggles and hardships they face.

Some may wonder, "Why worry about the future when tomorrow is not promised?" But in my opinion, not knowing what the future holds is a perfect reason to be prepared. Do you think most of the elderly people still working well past their retirement age thought they would have to do so? You see, you can no longer use the excuse of not having the money or time to invest, or that it's too hard to invest. Can you really afford not to invest in your future?

"Government is not the answer. The answer lies in us. We alone are responsible for our ultimate financial welfare." —Robert G. Allen

INVESTING THE WORRY-FREE WAY

Before I tell you what worry-free investing is, let me tell you what it isn't. Worry-free investing is not a "get-rich-quick" investing program. I repeat: Worry-free investing is not a "get-rich-quick" investing program! It's a program that instructs investors how to use the principles and strategies of some of the world's best and most successful stock market pros to buy and sell stocks that enable the investor to build wealth in an intelligent manner over the long term. Some individuals may think worry-free investing means "risk-free," but that's not the case. worry-free investing, like most other investment plans or programs, also carries risks. It would be nice if it didn't, but I'm afraid that it's not possible to invest in so-called "risk-free" stocks.

If I didn't call this program "worry-free investing," I would probably call it "peace-of-mind investing." The peace-of-mind comes from knowing when I have created a portfolio, its creation is based on the tried-and-true principles and strategies used by the best minds in the investment business. Make no mistake about it, there will be some volatility to even a worry-free portfolio, and some picks will result in capital losses; but in the end, there should be a lot more winners than losers — and with those winners, the sky is the limit.

So, what exactly is worry-free investing? It's nothing new. Benjamin Graham, regarded by many to be the father of value investing, stressed the importance of having a margin of safety with every stock that is purchased. The same is true with worry-free investing. Jim Slater believes some of the best returns can be realized by investing in small- to medium-size companies that have shown strong historical growth in their earnings, and worry-free investing stresses the same. Warren Buffett would probably tell us to only invest in businesses that have a durable competitive advantage. Guess what? So, does worry-free investing. John Bogle, the father of the index fund, would probably tell us not to waste our time trying to time the stock market. Sounds a bit like worry-free investing to me. John Bogle has been an investor for more than sixty years! Peter Lynch, perhaps best known for achieving 29% annual returns during his 13-year tenure with the Magellan Fund, would probably tell us to only invest in businesses that we understand, to have patience and to not get scared out of the stock market if we truly want to make some serious money. That definitely sounds like worry-free investing to me. You see, worry-free investing is the incorporation of some of the best and most effective stock-investing strategies and principles of the world's most successful investment pros into one very effective investment program — though it is much, much more than that.

It's also about utilizing various investment tools, such as the Caps rating system developed by the Motley Fool, that have been created simply for the purpose of helping you and me become better investors. Then there are websites such as Gurufocus.com, Insidermonkey.com and Fool.com that I also consider to be tools, as their main goal is to educate investors. Worry-free investing also is about thinking outside the box, and using what works for you and discarding what doesn't. Finally, worry-free investing is about having a specific mindset or temperament. This book provides you with the principles and strategies that I have used to help me develop the temperament that is needed to succeed as an investor. It's something that either you have, or you must develop; and if you find that you already have the temperament, it sure wouldn't hurt to improve or strengthen it.

"Investing should be more like watching paint dry or watching grass grow. If you want excitement, take $800 and go to Las Vegas." —Paul Samuelson

CHARACTERISTICS OF A
WORRY-FREE BUSINESS

To invest like a stock market pro — i.e., a worry-free investor — you must see yourself as a business owner. Think about it: whenever you and I buy a stock, we actually are buying partial ownership in a business. So, our goal should be to locate and purchase the best businesses we can find. There are specific characteristics a worry-free business should possess that tell us it's capable of creating wealth for the investor over the long term.

A worry-free business should be fairly easy to understand. According to Peter Lynch, "If you're prepared to invest in a company, then you ought to be able to explain why — in simple language that a fifth-grader could understand, and quickly enough so that the fifth-grader won't get bored." Time and time again, research has shown complex investments tend to be poor investment choices.

A worry-free business needs strong brand appeal to give it a sustainable competitive advantage. (Just think of our mindset: many of us are particular about the brands we choose when purchasing certain items.) During a trip to the local mall with my wife and granddaughters a few years back, I remember walking into a teen clothing store and being amazed to see it was packed with teenagers and parents eager to spend their money. That event alone was enough to convince me the business definitely had strong brand appeal.

It is important for worry-free businesses to be investor-friendly and investor-oriented. We only want to own the stocks of businesses in which the managers, first and foremost, look out for the interests of its owners — because, as shareholders, that includes you and me. Just think of all the financial scandals we've seen wipe out the wealth their investors, like the Bernie Madoff Ponzi scheme, and the Enron and WorldCom scandals, to name a few. Going to sleep a millionaire and waking up broke has got to make for a bad day. So, we need to be certain the managers running the businesses in which we invest are sharp, trustworthy and investor-oriented (aka owner-oriented).

Cash is king. It takes cash to pay the bills, repay bank loans, compensate employees, purchase supplies and equipment, fund research and development, etc. If the money isn't there or coming in, don't expect the business to last. So, taking a cue from Jim Slater, a worry-free business should be a strong, positive free cash flow generator. The world's best businesses have proven to be strong generators of a positive free cash flow.

Finally, the worry-free business needs to be conservatively financed. As worry-free investors, we should only own businesses that carry little to no debt — or, more specifically, little to no long-term debt.

These five characteristics are the heartbeat of any worry-free investment that generates great wealth. Businesses that fail to meet all five criteria are not worthy of investment.

Five Characteristics of a Worry-Free Business

1. They should be fairly easy to understand.
2. They should have a strong brand appeal.
3. They should be investor friendly and investor oriented.
4. They should be positive, free cash flow generators.
5. They should be conservatively financed.

"Try to find a business that you can understand, that's not particularly complicated, that has a successful long-term track record, makes an attractive profit, and can grow over time." —Bill Ackman

TAKE THE CHALLENGE

On March 10, 1986, I entered the United States Marine Corps and began basic training at Parris Island, South Carolina. Not even in my wildest dreams could I have imagined what awaited my arrival. For about 12 weeks, other recruits and I were put through some of the toughest, most grueling training imaginable — at least, that's what I believe. It was not only physically demanding but mentally demanding as well. The drill instructors made life miserable for us, but I understood what they were doing was for my benefit and for the benefit of the other recruits. In Marine Corps basic training, 100% is never enough. You must push yourself beyond your limits because failure is not an option.

Some of my friends wanted to know why I chose the Marine Corps out of all the branches of service I could have entered. I told them I love a challenge, and I had been told that the Marine Corps had a really tough training program. (That's an understatement!) At the completion of basic training, I was one of three recruits in my platoon to graduate with Honors. I gave it my all and it paid off.

Perseverance was my key to success here, and it will be yours as an investor, too. Are you willing to take the challenge? You probably have heard the expression "knowledge is power," but I believe the saying is incomplete. I'm sure you know some people who are smart and knowledgeable in different areas of life, yet their lives are a mess. Well, knowledge is power, but it must be the right knowledge and it must be put into action. Don't just read this book and put it aside to collect dust. Take the challenge and put this information to use. Be a person of action!

"Everyone has the brainpower to make money in stocks. Not everyone has the stomach. If you are susceptible to selling everything in a panic, you ought to avoid stocks and stock mutual funds altogether." —Peter Lynch

INVESTING DISCIPLINE IS ESSENTIAL TO SUCCESSFUL INVESTING

The very first thing recruits are taught when they arrive at Marine Corps Recruit Depot Parris Island is the importance and the necessity of discipline. Discipline is instilled in the recruits throughout the entire basic training program to the point that its importance would be hard for any recruits to ever forget. Discipline is just that important for the day-to-day operations of the world's finest and fittest organization of fighting men and fighting women.

During my basic training many years ago, the drill instructors would give the command "zero" to my platoon. In response to the command, all recruits were required to immediately cease what they were doing, regardless of the activity, and would become perfectly still. It did not matter if we were taking a shower, shining our boots, cleaning our weapon or sitting on the toilet — we immediately froze in place and began to repeat the following statement in unison: *"Sir! Discipline is instant, willing obedience to all orders, respect for authority, self-reliance and teamwork Sir. Freeze Sir!"*

After completion of the statement, we remained completely still until we were given permission to move. Just as a great dedication to discipline is necessary during military service, it takes a similar level of dedication to discipline to obtain great success through stock investing. Throughout this section, I will refer to the discipline I'm talking about as "investing discipline" or simply as "discipline" to keep things simple.

Before going any further, let's consider investing discipline for a moment. Investors who have investing discipline are able to stick to their investment plans and strategies regardless of the fear or chaos that exists in the stock market. (As we would say in the military, they stay the course.) You may have the world's best investment plan or program for building wealth, but it will be of little to no value to you if you lack the discipline needed to stick with it when things look bleak or hopeless. Markets go up and markets go down, but it is the disciplined investors that use both events to their advantage. The truth is, without investing discipline, there's a high probability of failure somewhere along the line.

The world's best investment pros are head and shoulders above most other investors when it comes to remaining disciplined. Learning investment discipline is much like learning a new sport. Practice and repetition was my key to developing investing discipline, and I believe that the same would apply to most of you. After putting my investment plan into action, if I found myself straying from my plan, I would look it over again to remind myself what I should and shouldn't be doing. It's always important to keep in mind that the principles and strategies we're using were developed and proven by some of the world's most successful investors, and if we truly want them to work, we have to stay the course in good times and bad times. Every time I felt I was slipping in my discipline, I repeated the process. Remember, practice makes perfect.

Below is a list of some of the common mistakes undisciplined investors make, which must always be avoided by the disciplined investor:

- Failing to stick to an effective plan or strategy
- Attempting to predict or to time the stock market
- Allowing fear and greed to control them
- Having unrealistic expectations about their investments and the stock market
- Lacking patience
- Failing to do their own research
- Investing with a short-term mentality
- Focusing on trying to get rich quickly
- Making investment decisions with their emotions
- Acting on speculation about a company or business
- Adopting a "herd mentality" by following the crowd
- Failing to practice investment discipline

Although the list isn't long, it could have easily been much longer, but I believe you get the picture. Above all else, remember to practice, practice and practice investing discipline.

"It is one thing to have a powerful strategy; it's another to execute it." —David Dreman

FINDING EXTRA MONEY TO FUND YOUR INVESTMENT PROGRAM

Most people who think they don't have the money they need to start investing usually actually do. The situation simply boils down to being smarter with the income they presently earn. When we begin to take a serious look at the situation, most of us have areas in which we are wasting money. This wasted money could instead be used to put us on a path to a worry-free, financially secure future.

Here are some ideas or suggestions on where to find that extra money to start your investment program.

1. Participate in your employer's sponsored retirement plan such as the 401(k), 403(b), or SEP (Simplified Employee Pension plan).

By contributing as little as 5% of your gross pay into your retirement plan, you are on your way to building a serious nest egg and at the same time you will reduce your taxable income. In no time at all, you will not even miss the contributions and will simply adapt to living on a little less income. In addition, your employer will usually match a percentage of your contributions, which actually gives you free money to invest and grow your wealth.

2. Invest your next pay raise.

When you receive your next pay raise, do not start spending it. Start investing it consistently and act as if it was never received.

3. Invest your next bonus.

Treat your next bonus as you would your next pay raise and invest it instead of spending it.

16

4. Invest your next tax refund.

Treat it as you would your next pay raise or bonus, as previously mentioned.

5. Increase your withholding allowances to bring home more money now.

If you find yourself receiving a large tax refund every year, you may be paying too much in income taxes throughout the year. A much better option would be to have less money withheld for taxes by increasing your withholding allowances. Most personnel departments can usually assist an employee with figuring out the correct amount of withholding allowances to carry. It's very important to compute the correct withholding allowances because you do not want to be stuck with a big tax bill when filing your income tax return.

6. Consolidate high-interest debts.

Consolidate high-interest loans and credit cards into a single loan with a low interest rate. Doing so should get you out of debt quicker and save you money in interest charges, too.

7. Pay off higher interest loans first.

If you are unable to or just do not want to consolidate your debt, concentrate your efforts into paying off higher interest loans first.

8. Make good use of earmarked money.

Once you have paid off a debt, do not start spending the additional money that becomes available. Take the extra income and use it to pay off other debts and to invest wisely.

9. Reduce the amount that you pay for prescription drugs.

If you or your family members are required to take prescription drugs, always ask for generics if they are available. Generic drugs must meet the same strict federal guidelines as name brand drugs and work just as well.

10. Buy straight term life insurance.

You don't need all the bells and whistles when it comes to life insurance. The main purposes of life insurance are to replace lost income and to pay off debts. When it comes to value and savings, a straight term life insurance policy is hard to beat.

11. Do not smoke or drink.

Both are very expensive and unhealthy habits that will cost you both now and later in terms of money and health. If you refuse to quit, at the very least, cut back drastically on these bad habits.

12. Do not purchase credit Life and disability insurance offered to you by the lending institutions.

This type of insurance is offered to individuals by banks and other financial institutions when they apply for a loan. It's supposed to pay the loan off if the borrower becomes disabled or dies. This type of insurance is not necessary, and the lenders cannot base their loan decisions on whether or not you purchase it. It's simply another way for financial institutions to make money since they rarely have to pay claims on this type of insurance.

13. Do not carry large life insurance policies on small children.

Never carry large life insurance policies on small children. Remember, life insurance's main purposes are to replace lost income and to pay off existing debts.

14. Purchase auto insurance and homeowners insurance at cheaper rates than you are currently paying.

When it comes to auto insurance and homeowners insurance, the cost varies among different agencies. Shopping around could result in savings of several hundred dollars annually in premiums.

15. Increase the deductible on your auto and homeowners insurance.

Increasing the deductible on your auto and homeowners insurance could result in savings of 20-30% in annual premiums.

16. Consider dropping collision and comprehensive coverage on older vehicles.

When a vehicle is worth only a few thousand dollars, consider dropping the collision and comprehensive coverage. Many people actually pay more in annual premiums than their vehicles are worth. It just does not make sense to do that.

17. Drive a fuel-efficient vehicle.

If you have more than one vehicle, drive the one that gets the best fuel efficiency. If you are considering buying a vehicle, purchase a good used one that gets good fuel efficiency.

18. Do not buy a new vehicle every few years.

If no major problems exist with your vehicle, get good use from it before committing to a new one and the payments that come along with it.

19. Cut up all credit cards except one.

Start paying cash for everything. You will find that when you pay cash for everything, you will be less inclined to spend your hard-earned money or to waste it on items that you do not need. Using several credit cards will keep you in debt forever. Cut up all credit cards except one, and use it only for true emergencies such as an auto repair bill or an insurance deductible.

20. Get rid of unnecessary bank and credit card fees.

If you pay annual fees for your credit card, switch to a low interest card that charges no fees. If you're also paying banking fees, rid yourself of them by talking with the bank's management and requesting that the fees be waived or lowered.

21. Stay away from ATM machines.

Get rid of the ATM cards and debit cards or use them as little as possible. ATM cards and debit cards make it too easy and convenient to access and spend your hard-earned money.

22. Carry your lunch to work.

Carry your lunch and other snacks to work. Doing so can easily result in savings of several hundred dollars annually.

23. Do not eat out.

If you are going to eat out, do so only on special occasions. A night out with the family could easily cost you more than a hundred bucks, so prepare and eat your meals at home.

24. Do not play the lottery.

Playing the lottery is like flushing money down the toilet. You will never see it again. Put your money into an excellent selection of stocks, mutual funds or index funds instead.

25. Get rid of unnecessary phone services.

If you find yourself with costly phone services that you do not use, get rid of them. It's a known fact that phone companies push extra services on the consumer knowing the services will hardly be used. Phone companies love it when you purchase those services since they cost them very little but bring in large profits. If you use a cell phone, be sure to sign up for a calling plan that has excellent terms, such as free minutes and low monthly payments.

26. Cancel cable or satellite television.

Get rid of the expensive cable or satellite television that continues to increase in cost year after year. Install a good digital antenna that provides you with several local and regional channels to view. If you insist on keeping your service, get rid of everything except the basic package.

27. Rent movies or join a video rental club.

Rent movies instead of going to the movie theater. If you think that the admission is expensive, just wait until you pay for the popcorn and drinks.

28. Look for forms of free entertainment for the family.

Most towns, cities and counties sponsor free forms of entertainment for the entire family. Check with your city and county government to see what free events are scheduled. These activities can be both fun and educational.

29. Get rid of the mini warehouse.

Make room at home to store your items or hold a large garage sale. Many times, the annual expense of renting the mini warehouse cost more than the items being stored are worth.

30. Drop the fitness center membership if it's not being used.

If you have not used the fitness center within the last year, then you probably won't. Find creative ways to exercise at home.

31. Conserve energy.

Make your home more energy efficient by properly insulating the attic, installing a programmable thermostat, using energy efficient light bulbs and talking with your local utility service provider for recommendations on how to conserve energy. When you conserve energy, you save money.

32. Get a part-time job.

If necessary, find part-time work and use the income from it to start your investment program.

These are a few simple and effective ways of finding extra money to invest. These are areas we take for granted and most of the time we don't even realize how much money we really are wasting. Implementing some of these recommendations could easily uncover several thousand dollars in real money for investing. The individual with the millionaire's mindset is the one who's willing to sacrifice now in exchange for future wealth.

"Financial peace isn't the acquisition of stuff. It's learning to live on less than you make, so you can give money back and have money to invest. You can't win until you do this." —*Dave Ramsey*

THE FINANCIAL PLANNER

I decided before I went any further, now would be a good time to discuss the financial planner. Wikipedia defines a financial planner as: *"A financial planner is a professional who prepares financial plans for people. The financial plans often cover cash flow management, retirement planning, investment planning, financial risk management, insurance planning, tax planning, estate planning, and business succession planning."*

I have never used financial planners but have seriously considered using them because I believe a good financial planner can be very helpful because of the various types of financial advice they can offer, plus the fact that a good financial planner can get you headed in the right direction when it comes to your finances.

I would be the last person to tell anyone not to seek the advice of professionals in areas of need because those professionals serve very important purposes just as a doctor serves a very important purpose in a medical emergency. The question that you must ask yourself is, "Do you really need the services of a financial planner or can you accomplish your desired financial goals without them?" The steps in the planning process financial planners use usually involves them setting goals with the client, gathering relevant information on the client, analyzing the information that was gathered, constructing a financial plan based on the gathered information, implementing the strategies in the plan, and monitoring the implementation of the plan. The most important benefit that an individual can receive from the use of a financial planner is the financial plan itself! Few people ever bother to develop a financial plan. Financial planners provide advice in many areas such as taxes, estates planning, retirement, insurance and risk management. So, in reality, a good financial planner creates a financial plan specifically tailored to you, then lays out step-by-step directions demonstrating how to achieve the goals of your financial plan. I also have learned that a little boost from others is what it takes to get some people going. Perhaps a financial planner is the little boost you need to get started.

The fees charged by financial planners vary from reasonable or extremely high. If you decide to use a financial planner, be sure to find out the fees you would be charged in advance, then decide whether they are fair for the services offered to you. If I were to hire a financial planner, I would only want to deal with one who charges an hourly rate or a flat fee for the services I receive, and would definitely stay away from those that are paid on commissions from financial or insurance products that they offer.

If you decide to hire a financial planner, do your homework before selecting one, as laws and requirement vary in different states about who qualifies as a financial planner. When hiring a financial planner, verify that he or she is a Certified Financial Planner® or CFP®. The Financial Planning Association® would probably be the best place to start.

"When it comes to investing, my suggestion is to first understand your strengths and weaknesses, and then devise a simple strategy so that you can sleep at night!"
—Walter Schloss

INVESTING IN THE INFORMATION AGE

We are in what is known as the "Information Age" thanks to the vast quantities of information available to the general public today. Even more amazing is how quickly information can be obtained or accessed simply by visiting your local library or by use of a computer. Think about it: just about everything we do can now be done online. We have banking, shopping, medical services, grocery purchases, investing and thousands of other services that can now be performed online. Not so long ago, the intelligent investor would have had to sort through numerous financial statements and reports just to get an idea of a company's operations. If the company seemed attractive enough, more research would be necessary. This research entailed looking at more company data, financial statements and reports, and whatever else the investor deemed necessary to get an in-depth knowledge of the business and its performance. To complicate matters, several years of the company's financial history would be needed for the research. Most investment experts are quick to acknowledge that Warren Buffett is a genius and there are very few people that would dispute that. Can you imagine the amount of time and energy that he must have put into researching just one company that he was interested in when information was not as freely available as it is now? It boggles my mind to think about that.

We can now retrieve in minutes or seconds the same type of information that Buffett probably spent countless hours locating, retrieving, researching and reviewing. Let's face it: we have innumerable resources available for reference when wanting to learn almost any subject. We just have to be willing to put in the time and effort to learn it. Sadly, the vast quantities of information available can overwhelm an individual, leaving him or her confused or intimidated.

I want to mention I have never used annual reports, 10-Ks, or what I consider to be very complex financial statements to determine whether or not to buy a stock and don't ever plan to. Although I have a very good understanding of complex accounting statements because of my business studies in college, highly technical accounting skills are not needed for us to succeed as investors. I do, however, take a look at mailings such as annual reports and 10-Ks I receive for stocks I already own though. Doing so allows me to be more informed concerning those investments.

I mentioned in the beginning of this section we are in the Information Age. So, why not use it to our advantage by letting other professionals do all the deciphering of the complicated financial mumbo jumbo for us. When I'm doing my research and analysis of stocks, I use the internet to obtain financial reports that have been prepared by intelligent financial professionals who are much smarter than I am. Now let me amaze you. The professionally prepared reports that I use are free! Isn't it great to be living in the Information Age?

"The underlying principles of sound investment should not be altered from decade to decade, but the application of these principles must be adapted to significant changes in the financial mechanisms and climate." —Benjamin Graham

INVESTING INTELLIGENTLY

According to research, more than 90% of actively managed funds fail to outperform the return of the overall stock market. When I first began doing my research for this book many years ago, that figure was 75%. It's amazing how the tables have turned. Gary Kaminsky, author and successful Wall Street money manager, stated in his book *Smarter than the Street,* "Taking personal control of your financial future makes more sense now than ever before." Additionally, he stated, "Research shows that in the last two plus decades, the percentage of money managers that beat the S&P 500 is down by a significant margin over the percentage for the decades prior to 1987."

Mutual funds, hedge funds and other investment funds are the pooling of money from several individuals and/or organizations into stocks, bonds, money market instruments and a variety of other types of equities with the goal of earning a profit. The funds raise money for investment purposes from the issuance of fund shares. The individuals or teams managing those funds are experts in their fields that use very powerful and sometimes complex investment tools to assist them with investment decisions; yet, most funds still fail to outperform the overall stock market. If that be the case, then it would seem that the small investor does not stand a chance of investing successfully in the stock market, but that belief could not be further from the truth.

So, why do the fund managers and other money managers fail so badly at their job? Simply because most managers exert too much effort and energy into always being invested in the hottest stocks at the moment. This is done in hopes of obtaining a quick, large profit from the investment. Along with this investment strategy comes an increased exposure to risk, because what's usually hot today won't be hot tomorrow! The small investor or individual investor must think long-term if he or she is going to achieve excellent returns from investing in stocks. Short-term investing in the stock market is just too risky. Although the stock market can be very volatile and unpredictable in the short-term, it's much more predictable over the long term.

The intelligent investor should purchase a stock with the intention of holding it no fewer than 10 years, according to Warren Buffett. In doing so, exposure to risk is decreased and personal feelings and emotions are kept out of the market, allowing the small investor to be positioned for excellent future investment returns. It's also very important to take a nontraditional approach to investing. Don't do what everybody else is doing and don't buy or sell a stock because everybody else is doing so. If you and I fall into the trap of doing what everyone else is doing, it's almost guaranteed that the performance of our investment portfolios will be just like everyone else.

The most successful investors have been those that run to the stock market when everyone else is running from it. They buy stocks that everyone else is dumping and dump stocks that everyone else is buying. They are happiest when the stock market has been beaten down or when there's a big market correction or when panic selling is going on in the market. They know that it's in times like those that the stocks of outstanding businesses can usually be purchased at a serious discount to their intrinsic or fair value. Remember, when pessimism is at its greatest, the most opportune times present themselves for making a lot of money by investing in stocks. In his book *Common Stocks and Uncommon Profits,* Philip A. Fisher states, "The wise investor can profit if he can think independently of the crowd and reach the right answer when the majority of financial opinion is leaning the other way." In gathering my research for this book, I found that all of the great investors were unique and nontraditional in their approach to investing. They simply refused to follow the crowd. If you would do the same, you are really investing like a stock market pro, and the results will speak for you.

"If you have good stocks and really know them, you'll make money if you're patient over three years or more."—David Dreman

TODAY'S YOUTH AND INVESTING

Throughout my childhood, I was never taught much when it came to budgeting, managing my finances, or investing. In those days Americans in general were taught to get a good job, work hard, and save money, and by doing so everything should work out alright in retirement. Well, when I look at our elderly population today, things have not worked out for the majority of them when it comes to their finances. Most are struggling and still living from check to check except instead of it being a paycheck, it's usually a Social Security check. Now, there's nothing wrong with receiving a Social Security check. As a matter of fact, I look forward to the day, if God permits, when I will begin receiving one myself. That is, if the government can get its act together concerning Social Security and the insanely high national deficit that we carry as a nation.

The mistake that Americans have made is in their failure to save and invest enough money in preparation for their retirement and it seems that our youth population is making the same mistake. Our youths are much smarter than my generation and all the generations that have preceded them except in the area of their finances and investing. When I consider today's youths, it is easy to see that they have so many advantages in comparison to previous generations. For example, it's much easier for most to graduate with a high school diploma when compared those generations that preceded them that were only allowed to attend school when the weather was bad. It's true! There was a time in our history when children were required to stay home and work the farm instead of attending school. I know because I have talked with many of those senior citizens and many of them cannot read. When the weather was good, they had to farm or work other laborious jobs to help the family. Literally, they had to work to eat. The youths of today would hardly find themselves in such harsh circumstances; yet, many of our youth are still dropping out of school when a good education is more important now than it has ever been. Our government has created an assortment of programs and incentives to encourage our youth to attend and to stay in school and yet more than 1.2 million students drop out of high school every year here in the United States.

Another advantage available to our youth that was not available to me in high school is the high-quality investment courses that most public and private schools now offer. In addition, the teachers, professors, or instructors are well qualified to teach our youth what they need to know to invest successfully in the stock market. Even more amazing to me is the fact that a large percentage of our public and private schools have investment clubs. So, I speak directly to all of America's youth that may be reading this book and say to you that you take some of those financial and investing courses offered at your schools. Join that investment club that you have been curious about. Talk to those instructors, professors, and teachers overseeing those programs and courses and learn from them everything that you can while you are still young.

If you would learn to sacrifice now when it comes to all of those material things that don't last or that will get old and start investing now, there's absolutely no reason why the majority of you could not obtain financial security and wealth in your 40s or sooner and that's a fact. Bernard Kelly, the author of *Flipping Burgers to Flipping Millions* is the perfect example of what our youth can achieve at a very young age. After graduating from high school, he went straight to work for McDonald's cooking fries and by the age of 30, he was a millionaire. Amazingly, he achieved this by working only at McDonald's and by investing only income that he earned at McDonald's. Our youth can achieve amazing things, if we encourage them and let them know that they can do it! Lastly, I speak again directly to our youth that you pay attention to those instructors, professors, or teachers and learn how to invest the right way. Learn how to invest the worry-free way and when you retire, perhaps that Social Security check may just be the equivalent of pocket change for you to use when you splurge a little.

"Learn how to take your losses quickly and cleanly. Don't expect to be right all the time. If you have made a mistake, cut your losses quickly as possible." —Bernard Baruch

THE POWER OF COMPOUNDING

The reinvesting of all income that's earned from investing results in your money growing. This growth is known as compound growth. Compound growth is what allows an investor to take a small sum of money and in time become extremely wealthy. It has been called the "Eighth Wonder of the World." All great investors relied or rely on the power of compounding to grow their wealth. I remember reading an article in an issue of *USA Today* that stated that Warren Buffett was worth an estimated $59 billion at that time. Do you think he invested half that amount to grow his wealth to that point? No way! Buffett originally talked family members and friends into contributing to his investment fund and initially raised about $105,000. Those one $105,000 have now grown to hundreds of billions of dollars in real wealth. Only after people began to see how successful he was as an investor, did more become interested in investing money into his investment fund. At the time of this writing, Berkshire Hathaway's stock is trading at well over $100,000 per share for its Class A shares. As far as I know, there's not a share of stock anywhere in the world that comes even close to its trading price. If a person had bought just 10 shares of Berkshire stock for a mere $300 or less in the late sixties once Buffett was at the helm, he or she would be a millionaire now from that small investment. With Warren Buffett, we see the power of compounding at its best in the hands of the World's Greatest Investor. It doesn't take a lot of money for you to achieve great wealth. It's just important that you get started investing now and let the power of compounding work for you.

Following are two examples to allow you to see the difference between a fixed return on an investment of $10,000 with the annual profits not reinvested and that same investment with the annual profits reinvested for a compound return.

Example 1

Original Investment Amount $10,000
Annual Return Percentage 10%
(Profits Not Reinvested)

YEAR	PROFIT
1	$1000
2	$1000
3	$1000
4	$1000
5	$1000
6	$1000
7	$1000
8	$1000
9	$1000
10	$1000

Total Profit $10,000
Original Investment $10,000
Ending Balance $20,000

Example 2

Original Investment Amount $10,000
Annual Return Percentage 10%
(Profits Reinvested)

YEAR	PROFIT
1	$11000
2	$12100
3	$13300
4	$14641

5	$16105
6	$17716
7	$19487
8	$21436
9	$23579
10	$25937

Total Profit $15,937
Original Investment $10,000
Ending Balance $25,937

By reinvesting all profits, an investor would end up with $5,937 or about 30% more money than he or she would have if the profits had not been reinvested. The power of compounding becomes even more potent over a longer period of time and when an investment's returns are greater. What I have learned from studying the world's best investors is that it is possible to obtain growth rates of 12%-15% or more annually by investing in stocks. Obtaining those types of returns take time and patience. It also takes a willingness on your part to allow stocks to meet your desired purchase price before buying them, even when those stocks are already trading at very attractive prices. It's going to take purchasing the right stocks and holding them throughout the turmoil of the stock market. It also means buying stocks that are usually out of favor with most other investors. As you can see, the power of compounding is an essential component for investors wanting to build great wealth, and it should not be taken lightly.

Section update: As of the close of the stock market on June 9, 2017, Berkshire Hathaway's stocks closed at the trading price of $254,965 per share and Warren Buffett's net worth was estimated to be $73.8 billion.

"Investors that do the best, and have done the best, are those that stay and compound at above-average rates over the long term." —John Paulson

INTERESTING FACTS ABOUT INVESTING

When it comes to investing, what you know or don't know can make you or break you, literally. It is very important to know the facts when investing in stocks and not knowing the facts will likely lead to poor investment decisions and poor investment choices, which will likely lead to poor investment returns or losses. In this section, I address risk, stock market volatility, day trading, recessions, margin accounts, and stock splits since it seems that many individual investors have the greatest misconception about these items and really need to have at least a basic understanding of them.

RISK: There are very few investments that are completely free from risk and all stock market investing carries some degree of risk. The main risk is the loss of your hard-earned money. So, the next time you hear someone pushing some sort of risk-free investment you should be very suspicious of them. Your goal as an investor should be to reduce risk as much as possible. This is not achieved by picking safe, conservative stocks, but by picking stocks of outstanding companies and buying those stocks at the right price, and selling them when it becomes necessary. I will definitely talk more about risk later.

STOCK MARKET VOLATILITY: A stock's price may fluctuate greatly within a short period of time even though nothing has fundamentally changed about the business. There are times when the stock market is calm and there are times when it's very volatile. Volatility is a normal process in the functioning of the stock market and should be expected. Stock market volatility is really a reflection of investors' perception of what is going on with the economy. Successful investors understand that the stocks they buy may fall 50% or more in value, but they know not to panic and sell their shares in the process. Instead, they continue to focus on investing for the long-term. For example, Warren Buffett began buying shares of USG Corp. in 2006 at an average price of $46 to $47 per share. After his purchase, the shares fell as

34

low as $4 per share at one point. At the time of this writing, the shares are still in Berkshires Hathaway's portfolio; although many years have passed, and the shares have recovered somewhat. Getting scared out of the market is what keeps most people from making any sizable returns.

DAY TRADING: It is the process of buying and selling stocks based on what an investor perceives that the market will do next. To put it simply, the investor is trying to time the market. Attempting this may be based on some information or rumor that the investor has heard or received. It has got to be one of the worst and most dangerous stock trading practices in existence. It should be called death trading because using it is certainly going to kill your wealth. Most day traders rid themselves of all stock purchases the same day that they buy them, even if it means that they will sustain heavy losses in the process. I read that John Bogle said that he did not know how to time the stock market. He said that he has never met anyone who does, nor has he ever met anyone who knows anyone who does. What a statement to be coming from an investor of his caliber. Bogle has been investing for more than 60 years. Do you get the picture? Never day-trade or attempt to time the stock market. We will discuss day trading again later since it is such a prevalent practice that destroys wealth instead of building it.

RECESSIONS: During recessions, most investors flee from stocks and move their money into what they consider safe havens such as U.S. Treasuries, high-grade bonds, money market accounts, and cash. What they don't realize is that recessions and other economic woes are usually the best time to purchase stocks. Usually at some point during a recession, most stocks will trade at prices far less than they are worth. I'm talking about their intrinsic value or fair value when I speak of worth. Not surprising, you may find stocks trading at just 20-25% of their intrinsic value. When it comes to investment value, it does not get any better than finding deals like that.

MARGIN ACCOUNTS: A margin account is a credit line provided to you by your broker to use for investment purposes; the amount of the credit line is based on the value of your brokerage account. Most margin accounts allow you to have a credit line equal to the balance in your brokerage account. For example, let's say that you have $10,000 in your brokerage account. The margin account will usually allow you to purchase up to $20,000 in stocks, mutual funds, or other investments offered on the stock exchange. This is one time that you should not use OPM, or other people's money. Never use a margin account for investing in the stock market, and my reason for recommending that you don't is a good one. Stocks are too volatile over the short-term.

Imagine this: You have just used your $10,000 plus the $10,000 credit line from a margin account to buy 2000 shares of a stock trading at $10 per share. Within a few days or weeks, the stock falls to $5 per share. How much money do you have left in your account that belongs to you? The answer is NONE!!! You have lost all of your money. Remember, the other $10,000 belongs to the broker. There's also another drawback. Since you no longer have $10,000 and the broker no longer has your investment as collateral, he is going to demand that you put more money into the account as a cushion to protect him from losses, which is known as a margin call, but he's going to require this before you even come close to losing 50% of your account's value. I know that the example that I just presented you with is a little on the extreme side, but you need to understand that with margin accounts, your losses double. Now, this is just one example of the dangers of using margin accounts. If instead, you had bought 1,000 shares of the same $10 stock using only your money and it fell to $5 per share, you would still have $5,000 in stock. With margin accounts, you can lose money even on excellent stock choices because even excellent stocks will tumble in price. My greatest capital losses were the result of foolishly using a margin account, so stay away from them.

STOCK SPLITS: By definition, a stock split is the division of a share of stock into more shares that leaves the total value of the shares unchanged. For example, if a company announces that it has an upcoming 2-for-1 stock split for its shares, that means that for every share that an investor owns, he or she will receive two new shares that replace the original share. In other words, 100 original shares become 200 new shares. Although the share price will change, the total value of the shares will not. When I was new to investing and very ignorant of what I was doing, I was always chasing after stocks that were about to split. The only thing a split does is lower the trading price of a stock. What really matters is the business itself and how it's performing. None of those stocks that split after my purchase performed any better after they split. Wall Street would have you to believe that splits are important, but they really are not. So, don't chase after stock splits because doing so is just a waste of time, and you definitely won't get any richer from the process.

"90% of the people in the stock market, professionals and amateurs alike, simply haven't done enough homework." —William J. O'Neil

RECESSION: ISN'T THAT GOOD NEWS?

Although I have already talked about recessions, I wanted to address them just a little more since recessions present the best opportunities for you to find undervalued stocks. The Great Recession that we recently experienced was the worst recession seen since the Great Depression. Even to date, the economy has not managed to fully shake its effects. The Great Recession started with the housing bubble in 2007 and turned into a global recession that had lasting effects throughout the whole world. It affected rich nations and poor nations. It seems that no one anywhere was immune from the damage it caused.

I learned from my study of Psychology that the "fight or flight" response is a part of the human psyche and can be expected of any person when there's a sign of trouble or danger. So, it's understandable when we see most investors fleeing to what they perceive to be safety when they learn that we have entered a recession because it has been said, "We are wired that way." Sadly, the flight mentality does more harm than good for most of those investors that respond in that manner. I will admit that recessions are dreaded by most people. Stocks get beaten and battered, people lose jobs, homes get repossessed, investment portfolios go down into the dumps, and panic generally sets in for many individuals, especially investors. Even outstanding businesses see their stocks drop in value along with everyone else. What we should do is look at recessions as speed bumps that serve the purpose of getting our economy out of danger and back on track when something's not right. Here's the good news. Recessions don't last forever. We have experienced eleven, that's right, eleven recessions since the Great Depression and our country has rebounded from every one of them to become a stronger and more prosperous nation. Investors with the courage to put their money in the market during recessions have usually been rewarded very well. Just imagine, they were running to the market while everyone else was fleeing it. What recessions do for the investor is present a great opportunity to buy the stocks of great businesses at a big discount in comparison to their fair value. Going against the herd, I purchased some excellent stocks during the Great Recession, and I have earned some excellent returns on those investments.

During recessions, you can expect to see stocks trading at true bargain prices. Many excellent stocks may fall as much as 75-80% in price. Although recessions are a common occurrence, seeing your 401(k) or stock portfolio's value slashed in half does not feel so common. During the Great Recession, there were many people that joked that their 401(k)'s had become 201(k)'s. A stock's performance data resulting from a recession does not reflect the true, long-term performance of a business and investors need to be careful of how they use the data. During my approach to investing, I am cautious concerning the use of a company's financial data created during recessions and make what I believe to be common sense and appropriate modifications to my stock analyses when necessary.

Again, I must stress that recessions present your best opportunities to find undervalued stocks. Investors that fail to invest during recessions are making a serious mistake. I also want to mention that market corrections and panic selling present good opportunities to find stocks trading at big discounts to their fair value but to be prepared for the situations mentioned you need to make sure you have a cash reserve set aside specifically for that purpose.

"People invariably feel better after the market gains 600 points and stocks are overvalued and worse after it drops 600 points and the bargains abound." —Peter Lynch

THE AMAZING IRVING KAHN

Since this book is based almost entirely on the principles and strategies of some of the world's best and most successful stock market pros, I thought that it would only be proper to talk a little bit about at least one I greatly admire, Irving Kahn, who is an American businessman and value investor. If Kahn tells us that he has "been there and done that," he will get no argument from me. After all, he was born on Dec. 19, 1905, and as of now; he's currently the world's oldest living investor and money manager at 109 years of age.

In 1928 Kahn started his career in the stock market with Hammerschlag, Borg & Co., and has lived through several major wars, the Great Depression, multiple recessions, stock market crashes, and the most recent Great Recession and has continued to invest throughout all of those events. Kahn still works at Kahn Brothers Group Inc., a privately-owned investment advisory and broker-dealer firm founded by him along with his sons, Thomas and Alan in 1978. Kahn currently serves as chairman of the organization that he helped found. He is a value investor who learned directly from Benjamin Graham himself, and he is Graham's oldest living student. Kahn is known to have a strict adherence to the value investing philosophies and principles that he learned from Graham. At Columbia University Business School, Kahn worked as a teacher assistant to Graham where they produced many famous students including Warren Buffett, who is considered by many to be the world's greatest investor.

According to a *Wall Street Journal* article, Kahn said that an important thing that he learned from Graham was the strength to resist the temptation to trade for a quick buck. In addition to being a teaching assistant to Graham, Kahn also contributed to Graham's popular and well-known book, *Security Analysis*. When looking at the Kahn Brothers' investment performance, according to a *Kiplinger Personal Finance* article written by Andrew Feinberg, from the beginning of 2000 through March 2014, the Kahn Brothers' picks have produced an annualized return of 11%, which beat the S&P 500 index by an average of 7.8 percentage points per year. In the same article, the Khans are described as ultra-patient value investors who often hold stocks for 20 years. Now, that's what I call long-term investing!

Next, I have made an attempt to list some of the principles that the legendary Kahn Brothers adhere to when investing in stocks. You will find that some elements surface again and again throughout this book and that's no coincidence since the world's best investors tend to have a lot in common when it comes to their golden rules of investing.

Invest for the long-term. Expect to hold a stock for a minimum of 3 to 5 years to reap the benefits of the investment. As I mentioned a moment ago, the Kahn Brothers have been known to hold some stocks for 20 years or more.

Insist on a margin of safety. Again and again, a margin of safety comes up when I research the methodologies of the world's greatest and most successful investors. A margin of safety is got to be there with every purchase.

Stay within your circle of competence. The Khans will only invest in businesses or industries that they understand. We would be wise to do the same.

Don't follow the crowd. The Kahns tend to be contrarians when it comes to their stock picks. They are usually buying what nobody else wants. As Philip A. Fisher stated in *Common Stocks and Uncommon Profits*, "The matter of training oneself not to go with the crowd but to be able to zig when the crowd zags, in my opinion, is one of the most important fundamentals of investment success."

Feelings and investing don't mix. When it comes to investing, feelings don't count. Keep your emotions out of the market.

Keep some cash in reserve. Having some cash, allows the investor to be prepared for the bargains that arise as the result of panic selling, stock market crashes, recessions, and other unforeseen events that cause stocks to tumble in price.

Avoid the use of leverage. Never use borrowed funds to invest in stocks or other securities. If you are investing on margin and the market drops, things can get very ugly and can take a turn for the worst very fast. I learned this lesson the hard way and it almost broke me financially.

Look for investor friendly companies. Prefer to invest in companies in which management holds a meaningful ownership stake. When management is at risk of a significant loss of wealth that's tied to the business, it tends to do a much better job of looking after the interests of all investors.

Know what a company is worth. Only by knowing what a company is worth can the intrinsic value of its stock be determined. The Kahns will usually sell a stock once it reaches their estimate of its intrinsic value.

Don't attempt to time the market. It's a task that has proven impossible to do, especially over the long term.

Go for the unpopular and out-of-favor. The unpopular and out-of-favor is usually where the best bargains can be found.

Look for companies with solid balance sheets and little to no debt. The Kahns like to invest in a company that's selling at a big discount in comparison to its assets and book value. They also like to see a stock trading at a low P/E ratio in comparison to its long-term average.

Accumulate shares gradually. The Kahns will buy a small position of a stock and add to the position as they get to know the company and its management better.

There is no doubt in my mind that this section barely scratches the surface when it comes to the investment methodology of the Kahn Brothers. Just think of all that Irving Kahn has seen, experienced, and learned in his lifetime. I recently lost a great uncle who was the patriarch of the family. He was born in 1917 or 1918 if I'm correct. He was a man loved and adored by his family and especially his nieces and his great nieces. He and I had many wonderful talks that were both fun and educational for me because even at his old age, his mind was sharp. One day, I remember turning to him and saying, "Unck, you are a living history book." And at the completion of my comment, he began to cry. I don't think that he had ever seen himself in that manner but after my comment, the thought must have really sunk into his mind. If my uncle was a living history book, what does that make the amazing Irving Kahn who at 109 years of age is still going strong?

It is my hope that his family and those that have the privilege of spending time with him realize what a rare and special treasure they have. He's an irreplaceable treasure to be sure. Once he's gone, there will never be another like him.

Section update: Mr. Irving Kahn died on Feb. 24, 2015, a few weeks after I wrote this section of the book.

"I would recommend that the private investor tune out the prevailing views they hear on the radio, television, and the internet. They are not helpful. People say, 'buy low, sell high,' but you cannot do this if you are following the herd." —Irving Kahn

PART TWO

THE GOOD, THE BAD AND THE UGLY — SYSTEMS, TOOLS, PRINCIPLES & STRATEGIES

BUILD A CASH RESERVE

If you are just starting out and are still in the process of building up your portfolio, you probably don't have the funds to set aside in a cash reserve, but this should be something that you consider later after you have built your portfolio up and extra cash becomes available. When I first started investing, my account was very small in value and I did not have the extra cash for building a cash reserve. Remember, I mentioned earlier that your main reason for needing one is to be prepared to purchase stocks when those amazing opportunities come along that are almost too good to be true. For example, in 2009, we could have purchased Harley Davidson Inc. for about $12 per share. At the time of this writing, Harley Davidson is trading for about $67 per share. If you and I had purchased it and were still holding it, we would be looking at a capital gain of 458%, plus Harley Davidson pays a quarterly dividend. Let's put it another way, had you or I put $5,000 into Harley Davidson, that $5,000 would now be worth $22,900 about five years later and that does not even included dividends that would have been received. So, you definitely want to build you up a cash reserve once you are capable of doing so because deals like that are going to come along every once in a while. Otherwise, you may have to sell other stocks in your portfolio to raise the funds needed for the purchase, but the worst part is that you may have to sell those stocks at a big loss. How much you decide to set aside is totally up to you but consider the amount you will invest in each stock and the maximum number of stocks you are willing to add to your portfolio. I keep things simple. I used to keep a cash reserve of about 10% of the portfolio's total value but now that reserve sits at about 20% of the portfolio's total value and that's where I plan to keep it for now. One last thing that I want to mention while I'm still in this section is that when I hear that the market has fallen several hundred points, I ask myself only one question and that is, "Are there any high-quality stocks on sale now?"

"Always keep a good part of your capital in a cash reserve. Never invest all of your funds." —Bernard Baruch

BUY-AND-HOLD INVESTING IS DEAD, NOT!

The strategy of buying and holding a stock for the long-term is dead! At least that's the argument that a lot of investment experts and financial analysts have been making since the Great Recession seemed to have stripped even the smartest investors of some of their wealth. I, for one, vehemently disagree with the notion that buy-and-hold investing is dead. I'm fully convinced that it is — and will be for some time to come — the best method to use for building wealth with stocks. A lot of professionals have been investing for a long time; yet, most of their success is no comparison to the success that Peter Lynch, Jim Slater, Charlie Munger, Lou Simpson, John Bogle, and other great investors have obtained. These men have proven that the long-term, buy-and-hold strategy is the ultimate way to build wealth. I'm willing to bet that many investment experts do not practice the strategy of buy-and-hold investing, which is why they fail to outperform the market. Those critics that have concluded that buy-and-hold investing is dead tend to look at a very limited timeframe or a very limited number of economic events. Drawing any conclusion from such a short period of time is wrong and downright ridiculous.

We have had eleven recessions since the Great Depression struck, but history has shown again and again that those investors that have bought and held on to stocks for the long-term through good times and bad times have usually done quite well when compared to the performance of the short-term investor. Philip A. Fisher, the famous growth investor and investing pioneer, was convinced that if enormous profits were to be made with the right stocks, it was essential that those stocks be bought and held for the long-term. As a matter of fact, Fisher was so convinced that the buy-and-hold approach was the best way to invest, that he had only three sell rules that he observed. That's right, three! Unfortunately, most of today's investors have more than three sell rules and I must admit that I fall into that group. In addition, Fisher applied what he called the "three-year rule" to every stock that he owned. Under the "three-year rule," he gave a stock three years to perform as he expected it to, and would only sell a stock when it failed to live up to his expectations at the end of the three years. The only reason he would ever sell a stock before the three-year period was expired was if its story had changed. In other words, he would sell before the three-year period was completed if his view about the company and its stock had changed for the worse, or he realized that he was wrong in his assessment of the company or its management.

So, what I'm really saying with the points that have been made here is that buy-and-hold investing is not dead but it's still alive and kicking. If maximum profits are ever going to be obtained through investing, history has proven again and again that stocks must be held for the long-term. One final point, buy-and-hold does not mean buy-and-forget. It's would be a serious mistake to forget or neglect your investments these days. There's too much that can happen with an investment. Today's star could quickly become tomorrow's stinker. Make no mistake about it, there will be times when you will need to sell a stock or some stocks because things do change and sometimes quickly!

"If investors are to make money consistently, what is required is a return to far-sighted, long-term investing. That is the only kind of investing that promises rational investors the greatest economic returns over the long haul." —Charles Brandes

INVESTMENT RISK

What is investment risk? The definition of investment risk that I like is the one that I found at Investopedia: "*The chance that an investment's actual return will be different than expected. Risk includes the possibility of losing some or all of the original investment.*"

There are different types of risk when investing in stocks. In an article titled "The 3 Types of Investment Risk," Joshua Kennon addresses business risk, valuation risk, and force of sale risk. To keep things simple, the main risk that I'm concerned with is the loss of our money through investing. Remember, I stated earlier that worry-free investing does not mean risk-free investing. Like any other stock investment program, there are no guarantees and you can lose money. Although I have had great success since 2008 putting to use the simple and straightforward information taught in this book, I'll be the first to admit that investing in stocks is risky and the risk that I'm talking about is losing money.

Worry-free investing is a system of investing in which investors are usually purchasing the stocks of faster growing small and mid-sized companies at attractive and discounted prices, however, investors should not limit themselves to the just the small and mid-sized companies but should be prepared to invest in companies of any size or market capitalization although Jim Slater stated, "the greatest profits can be realized by investing in small and medium-sized companies that have shown strong past earnings growth." History and research indicate portfolios comprising only these fast growers tend to be more volatile and risky than most other types of portfolios such as large-cap blue-chip stock portfolios, or portfolios that contain a combination of stocks and bonds. Worry-free investing reduces risk by teaching investors how to identify companies that meet specific criteria that is explained in this book, such as the stress test, which puts to use the strategies of some of the world's best and most successful investment pros. The stock market pro or worry-free investor looks only to invest in those businesses that have displayed a long-term history of solid and consistent performance. If a business has performed very well over the last 10 years, there's a high probability that it will perform just as well over the next 10 years. Of course, there are no guarantees.

Are there things that investors can do to further reduce risk to their portfolios? Yes, and tons of books have been written on that subject. Although I'm not a big advocate of Index Funds, they still serve a very important purpose within the portfolios of many investors by further reducing investment risk. Even Warren Buffett has said that some investors are better off putting their money into low-cost index funds such as the Vanguard S&P 500 Index Fund. He stated, "By periodically investing in an index fund, the know-nothing investors can actually outperform most investment professionals." I think Buffett's statement provides enough evidence that investing a portion of your wealth into an index fund is one way to reduce investment risk because of its low cost and the instant diversification it provides. Even the Motley Fool® staff believes that the index fund should be the foundation of a beginning or new investor's portfolio. In an article that I read, the Motley Fool staff stated, "Little wonder that we think index funds should be the foundation of your portfolio. But for now, we simply recommend that for every dollar you put into stocks, you roll the same amount into an index fund." Of course, there are other actions that investors can take to reduce investment risk within their portfolio, such as:

- Realize that there is no such thing as a risk-free investment program.
- Determine how much investment risk you can handle and operate within that perimeter.
- Only invest money that you can truly afford to lose.
- Don't invest any money that you will need within five years into stocks.
- Create a portfolio that is diversified and includes 10-20 stocks.

- Before buying a stock, make sure that it contains a large margin of safety.
- Do not participate in the frequent trading of stocks but invest for the long-term.
- Only invest in stocks that have been assigned a 4- or 5-star rating by the Motley Fool's Caps® community.
- Consider adding some conservative investments to your portfolio such as high-grade bonds, certificates of deposit, and money market funds.
- Don't buy stocks on margin or through the use of a margin account.
- Seek the advice of an investment professional with a proven track record of success.
- Create and use practice accounts before investing real money into stocks.
- Learn and apply the Twelve Essential Principles of the Stock Market Pro that are taught a little later in this book. Reducing risk is the most important purpose for which the principles were developed and for which they serve.

I want to also mention while I'm thinking about it that many investors confuse volatility and risk. Volatility is the fluctuations in a stock's price and other factors besides risk can result in a stock being highly volatile. Some stocks may display a lot of volatility, yet may not be as risky, as many of those stocks that have a history of low volatility. Remember, it's not uncommon for many stocks to fluctuate 50% or more in price in any given year and this includes the stocks of some of the best companies in America. So, be careful not to classify a stock as a high risk or low risk based only on its volatility or lack thereof.

In certain years you'll make your 30 percent, but there will be other years when you'll only make 2 percent, or perhaps you'll lose 20. That's just part of the scheme of things, and you have to accept it. —Peter Lynch

DAY TRADING: A HAZARD TO YOUR WEALTH

Day trading is an investment system in which a trader makes multiple trades throughout regular sessions of the stock market in an effort to make quick profits. The day trader will usually buy and sell a stock the same day and may own the stock for just a few minutes or a few hours. Usually at the end of the day, the day trader will sell out all open positions, even at a loss, to have money available for making trades when the stock market opens again. There used to be a warning on cigarette packs that stated, "Warning, cigarettes have been shown to be hazardous to your health." I have never smoked, and I have not bothered to see if the warning is still being placed on packs of cigarettes. We've learned about the harm that cigarettes cause those who smoke them. Day trading, like cigarettes, is also hazardous. It may not be hazardous to your health, but it's definitely hazardous to your wealth.

When I was just learning to invest, I experimented with day trading. I was up early in the morning trying to get the latest scoop on the next rocket stock that was going to propel me to great wealth, and I would literally sit at my computer from early morning to early afternoon performing research or buying and selling stocks. The only reason that I did not sit any longer than that was because I had a full-time job and had to go to work. I placed my buys and sells with excitement and sometimes I would win and sometimes I would lose. I found that if I had just held on to just about every stock that I sold at a loss through the reckless practice of day trading, I would have made money — and lots of it. Many of the stocks that I sold at a loss went on to double or triple in value over the next few years. Just think about that. I clearly didn't know what I was doing and yet if I had just held on too many of the stocks that I sold at a loss, I would have made profits of more than 100% on some and even 300% or more on a few. With a little patience, I would have done quite well as an investor. For example, I will never forget the time that I bought Devon Energy for $50 or $60 per share and sold it a few days later earning a $1 profit per share only to watch it jump more than $10 per share the day after I sold it.

What makes day trading so dangerous is the fact that the investor will mostly be losing money, but is so caught up in the trade that he or she convinces himself or herself that they can make the money back. Unfortunately, that is what happened to me. In just a very short time, I had a loss of $12,144 and the realizations of that loss floored me. I learned from that experience that day trading is a hazard to your wealth, and I no longer wanted to day trade, but wanted to find out what really works when it comes to investing in stocks. Even more, I decided that I would no longer spend all my time sitting at a computer in what proved to be a futile effort to find the next hottest stock, but decided that I would rather find some good, solid companies to invest in that would allow me some freedom from the stress and worry that comes with frequent trading. I decided that I would rather spend my time doing something more useful and enjoyable, like making money instead of losing it.

The big loss from day trading was an expensive education for me, but now that I think about it, I'm glad that it happened. It gave me the desire to find out what really works when investing in stocks, and for the next several years, I researched and studied everything that I could find about investing. What I have learned about investing in stocks is an accomplishment that I'm very proud of that started with me finding out that day trading is hazardous to your wealth.

"They find themselves switching in and out of stocks, feeding the brokers instead of themselves." —Charles Brandes

THE MOTLEY FOOL &
THE CAPS RATING SYSTEM

According to the Motley Fool® website, the Motley Fool is a multimedia financial services company that was founded in 1993 by brothers Tom and David Gardner. These two great investors' knowledge about investing is light years ahead of many of today's investors. I have read several of their books and articles. I have also listened to their television and radio appearances and to say that I'm always impressed with these amazing investors would be an understatement. I love their website, and I especially love the Motley Fool Caps® rating system that they have created to help investors pick top-performing stocks. I'm one that does not mind putting to use the old wise saying, "two heads are better than one," except that with the Caps® rating system, you are getting the collective wisdom of hundreds of thousands of brains that assign performance ratings to thousands of stocks contained in the Caps rating system. Stocks are rated from 1 to 5 stars with the coveted 5 stars being assigned to the stocks that investors believe will be the market's best performers and 1 star assigned to what they believe will be the market's poorest performers when compared to the performance of the S&P 500.

The Caps rating system is a very important part of my investment program that allows me to identify those hard-to-find top stocks that should outperform the market over the long term. I use the Caps rating system to confirm that the stocks that I have chosen are high quality ones that are favored by the Caps community also. First, I generate a list of stocks that meet my investment criteria set forth in this book, and then I verify that those stocks have been awarded 3 to 5 stars under the Caps rating system. I will usually try to purchase stocks that have a rating of at least 3 stars. To decrease risk even further, an investor can stick to purchasing stocks that carry a Caps rating of either 4 or 5 stars. To really understand how and why the Caps rating system works, visit the Motley Fool's website (fool.com) for a detailed explanation. If the Caps rating system is a regular part of the stock selection process, I truly believe it could turn the ordinary investor into an extraordinary one, and what would have been trivial stock returns into outstanding ones. When it comes to investing and making money in the stock market, the Motley Fool isn't FOOLISH.

"They don't have to, but most folks lose money. They commit three common mistakes: They overpay, buy businesses they don't understand and neglect to take a long-term approach. These three fatal errors account for most stock market failure." —*Kenneth L. Fisher*

GURUFOCUS.COM

GuruFocus.com is easily becoming one of my favorite go-to websites for investment information. It was founded in 2004 by Charlie Tian, an engineer and no doubt, an amazing man with an amazing mind. I'm not exaggerating when I say that the website is loaded with all kinds of good stuff to improve your investing skills and your returns on your investments. Wouldn't you like to see the most recent stock purchases of some of the world's most successful investors such as Ken Fisher, David Dreman, Lou Simpson, Joel Greenblatt, George Soros, Carl Icahn, Seth Klarman and many others? You can! Wouldn't you also like to take a good look at the holdings within those individuals' portfolios? You can! Wouldn't it also be nice to know what those great investors paid for specific stock shares contained within their portfolios? You can! Wouldn't you also like to know what the consensus picks are among those investors? You can! You can learn all of these things and much more at GuruFocus.com. You can also retrieve detailed performance histories of the great investors or look at financial statements for a specific company. The website also provides several financial tools that the investor can use free-of-charge and I really like the Fair Value Calculator.

Let me give you an example of the usefulness of this website. I have been considering purchasing shares of Gilead Sciences Inc., a research based biopharmaceutical company. Upon entering the stock symbol on GuruFocus.com and clicking the "Guru Trade," I found that Gilead Sciences Inc. has been purchased by Ken Heebner, Julian Robertson, Joel Greenblatt, John Rodgers, Ken Fisher and several other investors as of June 30, 2014. According to the website, Gilead Science's average trading price during the period was $77.76 per share. Do you think information like that could be very helpful to us? I could go on and on about how great this website is, but I won't. The website offers a vast amount of useful information and I'm amazed that so much of the information is currently free. Of course, there are some fee related services also offered, and there are limitations on some information available unless you subscribe to specific services offered by the website. When I consider GuruFocus.com, what's not to like about it? I love the website and if you take investing as serious as I do, I bet that you will too.

"You needn't be right 100% of the time to do well in investing. Rather, you want to aim to be right more than wrong." —Kenneth L. Fisher

INDUSTRIES AND
SECTORS WORTH AVOIDING

As a child, I was very active in sports, but it seems that I was never on a winning team in any of the sports that I played. Although we wanted badly to win, we never did. Now that I'm much older, I have drawn a conclusion from that time period that carries over into investing. The conclusion is that it's hard to win with a losing team. We weren't losers as in quitters, because we tried hard to succeed, but it appears that with every team that I played on, my teammates and I were just lousy when it came to sports. Well, when it comes to stocks, it's hard to win with a losing team. As you invest in the stock market, there are some industries and sectors that are best left to those that get a thrill from worrying and losing. It's probably best that you and I stay away from stocks in these industries or sectors because of the greater degrees of risk associated with them. Much caution should be exercised if you choose to invest in them. You will find the industries or sectors listed next with an explanation of why caution is in order.

Airline Industry: Their stocks are too risky since some airlines rarely make a profit, and they are subject to file for bankruptcy protection, which usually results in a complete wipeout for investors in their common stock. The most recent example is American Airlines filing for bankruptcy protection on Nov. 29, 2011. At the time of its filing, the airline had almost $30 billion in debt. Plus, the airline industry is a price competitive business, meaning that most consumers will make their selections based on the price of airfares and nothing else.

Automotive Industry: This industry is much like the airline industry in that it's also a price competitive one. With the purchasers of new vehicles, price is usually the most important factor that buyers consider when making a vehicle selection. We should be invested in businesses that have a durable competitive advantage that is the result of the products and services that they offer. Just think, if you want a Coca-Cola, you've got to get it through the Coca-Cola Co.

Commodities Sector: This sector is comprised of those businesses that deal in physical substances such as food, grains, metals, and energy products, such as oil and natural gas. This is a sector that is a great place to invest. That is, if you have a strong stomach for volatility. This sector is risky because it also contains mostly price competitive businesses. This sector is very volatile and will send the average investor running for the door when things look bleak. For example, Freeport-McMoRan Copper & Gold Inc. was trading as high as $127 per share in May 2008, but had fallen as low as $16 a share by December 2008. I will invest in commodities when the price is right because their volatility does not bother me, and the profits made are usually worth the wait, but commodity investing is not for everybody. If you are unable to handle your investment falling drastically in price, as was the case for Freeport-McMoRan Copper & Gold Inc., it's best that you stay away from commodities, because drops in price like that are common when one owns commodity stocks. Even with my own investment portfolio, I usually limit my purchase to one or two commodity stocks in a portfolio of twelve to fifteen stocks. Even then, they will probably be the smallest positions within the portfolio because it's just too easy to lose money investing in commodity stocks.

Telecommunications Industry: This sector deals with the transfer of information over great distances or areas for the purpose of communication. It includes cable, radio, television, cell phones, internet, and a multitude of other services. It's a complex and highly technical industry that is capital-intensive, meaning that telecommunications businesses have to spend large sums of money on items such as upgrades of their equipment and services. It's also a highly competitive industry. Telecommunications businesses are risky because it's easy for them to get left behind because of the invention of some new technology by a competitor that results in their business model being outdated. Research In Motion is the perfect example of a company that was a top dog not long ago, but other companies came out with better or cheaper replacements for their products. This is just one of those industries in which anything could happen. Nokia was another dominant manufacturer and service provider that has lost its edge to the competition. Other examples of telecommunications businesses are Verizon and AT&T.

Banks & Financial Institutions: They are complex entities that are hard for the average investor to understand. Peter Lynch and many other great investors seem to love them. I would recommend that you invest in them, but only if you really have a good grasp on how they function. It's also hard, if not impossible, for many investors to determine their intrinsic value. I owned a few bank stocks before the Great Recession struck and lost most of the money that was invested in them. So, I'm slow to invest in them, but I will if they meet the stringent requirements of the stress test explained later in this book. Even then, I'm likely to limit a portfolio of twelve to fifteen stocks to just one or two financial or banking stocks.

Technology Stocks: Don't avoid technology stocks, but make sure that they are a part of a well-thought-out and diversified portfolio. The main problems with technology businesses are that they tend to be very complex entities that are hard to understand and most always seem to be overvalued. I don't know about you, but I'm not going to purchase a stock trading at a P/E of 103, the P/E of Amazon.com Inc. at the time of this writing. I love good technology stocks and would not hesitate to invest in them, but here's the ticket: They must be seriously undervalued and not too hard for me to understand.

Foreign Stocks: This includes foreign stocks trading on American exchanges or foreign exchanges. Many foreign stocks are just too risky, and you don't really know what you are getting for your money. It appears that many Chinese and Indian businesses "cook the books" because of a lack of proper financial oversight that is common to companies and businesses located in the United States and Europe. There has also been a great deal of controversy concerning many Chinese companies that entered the U.S. market through reverse mergers. Two examples of the dangers of investing in this sector are Satyam Computer Services Ltd. and Longtop Financial

Technology Ltd., an Indian company and a Chinese company, respectively, that participated in fraud on a grand scale. If you want to invest in foreign markets, it's best to do so through U.S. companies that have a strong international presence.

OTC (Over-The-Counter) Stocks: These are stocks that are usually unable to meet the listing requirements of a formal exchange such as the New York Stock Exchange or the NASDAQ and are traded by broker-dealers via a dealer network. The OTC is also referred to as the "pink sheets" by some. Most of these stocks are highly speculative investments, which means they carry great risk. You are an investor, not a gambler, so stay away from them.

Penny Stocks: Don't believe all the hype surrounding penny stocks. Penny stocks are probably the world's most dangerous stocks to own. Most penny stocks are from new businesses that are just starting up. Those businesses are usually not even close to earning a profit and most never will. Their being called penny stocks is very suitable because if you invest in them, there's a very good chance that what you will be left with from your original investment is just pennies.

Although it's best that you avoid the industries or sectors previously listed, it may seem that I contradict myself on occasion because you may find that I own or have owned stocks from those industries or sectors. If that is the case, you can be sure that they have been included because they have long-term histories of being solid performers and reputable businesses. Let's just say that they are the best of the best in their industry or sector.

There may be other industries and sectors that require investors to exercise great caution that have not been mentioned here. What I want you to do is think before you invest your money into a company or business that you have some doubts about or that you are uncertain of concerning its financial condition or the integrity of its management. If you discover companies of the sort, finding somewhere else to invest your money is the most intelligent thing to do.

Section update – Nov. 17, 2016: The above assessment concerning the airline industry was written several years ago. Since that time, the industry has had a reversal in its performance and has performed very well as a group. The S&P 1500 airline industry group has a total return of 252% over the past five years. Over that same period many airline stocks have managed to grow their EPS at some very high rates. The fact remains that the airline industry is highly competitive and has a long history of bankruptcies, which has led many investors to mistrust the industry.

Although I have recently looked at some impressive financial information for several airline stocks, I could not harness enough courage to buy any of them.

"The only way one should buy stocks is if you understand the underlying business. You stay within your circle of competence. You buy businesses you understand."
—*Mohnish Pabrai*

TWELVE ESSENTIAL PRINCIPLES OF THE STOCK MARKET PRO

There are some principles that need to be adhered to if you want to truly invest like a stock market pro. Much research went into determining this list of twelve essential principles presented here. When studying and researching the pros, I found these principles to be universal among them, which means that these principles are essential and are not to be taken lightly although they may appear to be simple or common sense, yet the majority of those that invest in the stock market fail to use or obey them. Stick to them religiously and I believe that you will be pleased with the long-term results that they produce.

Principle #1: Only buy the stocks of businesses that you understand.

If you don't understand a business, don't purchase its stock. Investors are more likely to pick better performing stocks if they purchase the stocks of businesses that they understand. Usually those easy-to-understand, boring businesses are the ones that make money year after year. It has been said many times that a good investment is usually a boring one.

Principle #2: Invest for the long-term.

Warren Buffett has said that if you don't plan on holding a stock for 10 years, you have no business holding it for 10 minutes. Holding a stock for the long-term is the most effective way to maximize your return since a stock's earnings will usually increase dramatically over time along with its book value. These increases will result in the stock trading at a significantly higher price over the long term and if the stock pays dividends, the dividends are likely to increase consistently also.

Principle #3 Purchase stocks with low P/Es.

Look for stocks trading significantly below their average annual price-to-earnings ratio for the last seven to 10 years. The price-to-earnings ratio is normally referred to simply as the P/E ratio.

The equation that follows demonstrates how the P/E of a stock is determined:

$$\frac{\text{Price Per Share}}{\text{Earnings Per Share}} = \text{P/E Ratio}$$

For example, a stock is currently trading on the market for $40 per share. It has $2 in total estimated earnings for the year. The calculation would look like this:

$$\frac{\$40}{\$2} = 20 \text{ or a P/E of } 20$$

The P/E for the stock is 20. If this P/E is lower than the average annual P/E of the stock for the last seven to 10 years, then the stock is probably cheap based on what investors having been willing to pay for the shares in the past. I don't really get too excited until I see a stock trading at a P/E that's about half of its average annual long-term P/E.

Principle #4: Buy low and sell high.

Most investors tend to buy high and sell low, doing the exact opposite of what they should do. They buy an overvalued stock and when there's a market sell-off, they panic and sell too. This results in them selling the stock for much less than they paid for it. For smart investors, this market sell-off is a great time to buy excellent stocks at a discount.

Principle #5: Stay away from cheap stocks.

Everyone would love to be able to purchase a stock for $1 and watch it skyrocket to $40 before selling it, but that rarely happens. If a stock is very cheap or has recently lost most of its value, then something fundamental to the success of the business has other investors concerned. Look for undervalued, high-quality stocks instead of cheap stocks, and never buy a stock because it used to be $40 a share and now trades for $2 per share. If a stock's price has been on a continuous downhill slope and the stock has lost most of its value, think long and hard before purchasing it because there is probably something wrong with the business or at the business.

Principle #6: Select stocks that have strong brand appeal.

Look for companies or businesses that have strong brand appeal when purchasing stocks. Strong brand appeal gives them a durable competitive advantage over their competition. Examples are Nike, PepsiCo, Wal-Mart, Under Armour and Walgreens. Almost everyone has heard of these businesses or has purchased the products that they sell. When consumers see a brand name, they expect to receive high quality products at a fair price.

Principle #7: Create a portfolio that is diversified.

Diversification is one of the most important elements necessary for successful investing. When it comes to stocks, you should never put all of your eggs in one basket. Diversification reduces risk and improves an investor's opportunity for a better return. A diversified portfolio is one that consists of stocks from a variety of industries and sectors. For example, if you have decided to create a portfolio that will contain a total of five stocks, it would be unwise to hold five stocks from the same industry in that portfolio, such as five oil company stocks. The best and safest approach would be to purchase five stocks from five completely different industries. In doing so, if one or two of the industries suffer because of some economic turmoil, the other stocks should not be affected much or may not be impacted at all.

Principle #8: Keep your emotions out of the market.

Never make an investment decision that is based just on your feelings or emotions. Think about a scientist. A scientist is always concerned about the facts or the evidence that is present. You must be a scientist of the investment world. Always get the facts before buying or selling a stock. Emotions are the cause of a lot of the stock market's volatility, but when the underlying factors are checked, most of the time nothing notable has changed in the stock market that warrants the volatility.

Principle #9: Don't be greedy. (Unless others are fearful.)

Never allow greed to cause you to make very risky or foolish decisions when investing. Greed is the number one killer of an investor's wealth. Greed causes investors to make rash decisions without much thought or research. The smart investor is able to benefit from everyone else being greedy.

Principle #10: Do your own research.

Always do your own research to learn everything that you can about an investment. I believe that you can do a much better job managing your portfolio and finances than many of the investment experts out there. Remember, 90% of the fund managers fail to outperform the market. Unlike the investment adviser or fund manager that may have hundreds of accounts under management, you will only need to be concerned with your account and can therefore fully commit yourself to making the best choices and decisions concerning it.

Principle #11: Don't lose money.

This is exactly what's going to happen if you attempt to get-rich-quick or to time the market. When investing in stocks, you must be able to cope with your investments falling drastically in price without you panicking and selling your stocks at a loss. It's not uncommon for very good stocks to fall 50% or more in value in any given year, and that's definitely not something I enjoy seeing. If it happens to you, your response should be to hang on in there if you know that you have made the right choice. Better yet, buy some more of the stock if its fundamentals have not changed or have improved. Most importantly, have the goal and the determination to not lose any of your money from investing.

Principle #12: Be patient.

Just as Rome wasn't built in a day, the world's best investors did not amass their fortunes overnight. It took some time to do so. Time and the power of compounding are an investor's greatest allies. So, as you strive to build wealth, be sure to practice patience.

"Try not to let your emotions affect your judgment. Fear and greed are probably the worst emotions to have in connection with the purchase and sale of stocks." — *Walter Schloss*

THE ULTIMATE INVESTMENT VEHICLE

Although stocks are the ultimate investment for building wealth, I'm 100% convinced that the Individual Retirement Account, also known as the IRA, is the ultimate vehicle through which the individual investor should be investing in those stocks to augment the wealth building process. Many may argue that the 401(k) plan or some other employer-sponsored plan is the ultimate investment vehicle through which we should be investing. I think 401(k)'s are good but not great. I had one that ended up with much less money in it than I had actually contributed to the plan including the company's match. The biggest drawbacks to the use of 401(k) plans are the lack of control that the owner of the account has and the limited number of investments that are available within the account. Let me show you exactly what I mean. On two occasions, a company I worked for decided to change investment companies through which our 401(k) was provided and managed. On both occasions, the majority of mutual funds within our plans had fallen in value and most employees had lost money, but the losses were only on paper (unrealized). I went to our management on at least one occasion and expressed my dissatisfaction with the fact that their changing of investment companies was going to result in me — along with other employees — losing money. On both occasions, they changed firms anyway, and I lost a lot of money. Oh yes, the changes were done to save the company money — and it did, at the expense of its employees. The mutual fund choices offered by our plans were very limited and what I considered to be very poor selections. As a matter of fact, the plans had no index funds, balanced funds or money market funds in them. Now that's just sorry!

I'm not totally against 401(k) plans. One recommendation I made earlier in this book is to start contributing to your employer's sponsored retirement plan, which would include 401(k)'s, 403(b)'s, 457's, and various of other types of retirement plans. I would contribute enough to the plan to get the full company's match and no more, and the rest of my money that I want to invest would go into one or more IRAs.

What makes the IRA such an effective wealth builder are the tax advantages that it offers along with the control that the owner has over his or her account. Plus, an investor is almost unlimited when it comes to investment choices when using an IRA. Most brokerage firms offer IRAs. I use Scottrade®, a discount broker that charges very low fees for buy and sell transactions, and I have yet to be disappointed with the services they provide. My use of Scottrade is by no means an endorsement that you should use them, but I do recommend that you choose a reputable low-cost brokerage firm. Currently, there are two types of IRAs, the Traditional IRA and the Roth IRA, and we will provide some details on both types of accounts.

Traditional IRA: The Traditional IRA is a tax-deferred account, which means all contributions made to the account are made with pretax income and it reduces an individual's taxable income. Taxes are also deferred on all capital gains and dividends earned by the account. This deferring of taxes should result in a substantially larger nest egg for the investor since more money is available to invest. The Traditional IRA is available to all workers under the age of 70 1/2 at the end of the calendar year. Taxes become due at the time funds are withdrawn from the account. To avoid an early withdrawal penalty, an individual must be 59 1/2 years of age prior to making withdrawals and up to $10,000 may be withdrawn penalty-free to use for a first-time home purchase, but the withdrawal will be taxed as ordinary income. For 2017, an individual under 50 years of age can contribute total annual contributions of $5,500 and an individual 50 years of age or older can contribute total annual contributions of $6,500 to all IRAs owned. This account allows an unlimited annual rollover from another qualified plan. One last note, with the Traditional IRA, an individual whose income exceeds a specific limit may not be allowed to make tax deductible contributions to the Traditional IRA but can still make non-deductible contributions.

Roth IRA: The Roth IRA is an after-tax account because income taxes have already been paid on all money contributed to the account. All capital gains and dividends earned in the account are withdrawn tax-free if an individual has reached 59 1/2 years of age prior to making withdrawals. Making withdrawals prior to reaching 59 1/2 years of age will result in early withdrawal penalties unless funds up to $10,000 are withdrawn to use for a first-time home purchase. Single tax filers with modified adjusted gross incomes above $133,000 and joint tax filers with modified adjusted gross incomes above $196,000 are not eligible to use the Roth IRA. Although there are income restrictions to the use of the Roth IRA, there are no age restrictions as there are with the Traditional IRA. In addition, all contributions made to the Roth IRA can be withdrawn at any time without penalties since taxes have already been paid on those contributions. For 2017, an individual under 50 years of age can contribute total annual contributions of $5,500 and an individual 50 years of age or older can contribute total annual contributions of $6,500 to all IRAs owned. This account also allows for an unlimited annual rollover from another qualified plan.

There is much debate among financial experts as to which account is of the greatest benefit to the individual investor. I believe that for the individual investor, the Roth IRA is the better choice for those that qualify; and for those who don't qualify for the Roth, the Traditional IRA is the next best thing. I'm completely convinced that you and I can make a lot more money from investing than we would ever be required to pay in taxes, and this is why I prefer the Roth IRA over the Traditional IRA since no taxes are paid on withdrawals. Others may disagree with my belief and that's OK. For many, the Traditional IRA may just be the better choice, depending on the individual's circumstances. The income requirements and the contribution limits have tended to change annually for both the Traditional IRA and for the Roth IRA and are likely to continue to do so in the future.

To get started investing in an IRA, I would recommend that you contact a reputable brokerage firm such as Scottrade and request their information packages for both the Traditional IRA and the Roth IRA. Along with the information packages, you will also receive all the necessary applications to open the IRA. Once you have received the information packages, carefully read both of them to determine which IRA you qualify for and if you qualify for both, determine which IRA is the best choice for you. If you read both packages and are still unsure what to do, consult with a financial planner or other financial expert for help in this area because it can be a little confusing. Of course, with the use of a computer, most brokerages firms allow the necessary forms and instructions to be reviewed or printed from their websites. Finally, although I favor the Roth IRA, I'm certain that you can't go wrong even if you only qualify for the Traditional IRA. By the way, you can own both Traditional IRAs and Roth IRAs if you qualify for both types. Just remember that your total contributions allowed for one account also apply for other IRAs that you may own. For example, if you have two Traditional IRAs and one Roth IRA, and you are allowed an annual total contribution of $6,500, it means you are only allowed to contribute the maximum amount of $6,500 into all three accounts combined.

"Based on my own personal experience, both as an investor in recent years and an expert witness in years past, rarely do more than three or four variables really count. Everything else is noise." —Martin Whitman

THE STRESS TEST FOR IDENTIFYING TOP-PERFORMING STOCKS

This book's main purposes are to teach you how to invest and build wealth like a pro through a program of worry-free investing. Note that I said "worry-free," not "risk-free." When buying stocks, there's a right way and a wrong way to do so. Unfortunately, the wrong way is likely to leave you broke, busted and disgusted. When stocks are bought the right way, peace and happiness should be the final result along with a greater increase in your wealth. Buying the right stocks is just a part of the process, but those stocks must also be bought at the right price. Great joy comes over me every time I buy an excellent stock for much less than the stock is really worth. If you are old enough to remember, beginning in 2007 we experienced the worst recession since the Great Depression. During that recession, Treasury Secretary Timothy Geithner put some of America's largest and most powerful financial institutions through what was termed a "stress test." The stress test was supposed to provide him and the government with a clearer picture of the financial strength of each of those institutions. Likewise, I have outlined an eight-step stress test that I use to identify worry-free, top-performing stocks or in other words, the right stocks for building wealth. The stress test is based on the tried-and-true strategies of some of the most successful stock market pros.

STEP ONE. Check to see if the business has little to no long-term debt. If the business does have long-term debt, it should be capable of paying it off within five years out of its current annual profit.

Debt is an essential component in the operations of most businesses, but too much debt can be bad for a business. Too much debt reduces a business's profits, reduces the amount of money available for product research and development, and puts a business at greater risk of failure during a downturn in the economy. There are two items that I look at concerning debt and they are the debt-to-equity ratio and the debt payoff ratio.

Debt-To-Equity Ratio - This ratio compares the amount of debt to the shareholders' equity. Using this ratio, my goal is to find businesses that are worth more than they owe. The less debt a business owes, the more attractive it is to me. The debt-to-equity ratio can usually be found on any stock using one of the financial websites that provide financial data on stocks such as Morningstar.com. This website provides outstanding financial reports free of charge. When looking at stocks, strive to purchase stocks of businesses that have a debt-to-equity ratio of less than 1 and preferably much less than 1. The ratio tends to be less than 0.60 for stocks that I buy.

Debt Payoff Ratio - The debt payoff ratio tells us how many years it will take for a business to pay off its long-term debt out of its current annual profit. To calculate this ratio, divide the long-term debt by the current annual profit. A solid, fast growing business should be capable of paying off its long-term debt in five years or less.

The formula for the debt payoff ratio is:

$$\frac{\text{Long-Term Debt}}{\text{Current Annual Profit}} = \text{Debt Payoff in Years, Months, or Days,}$$

Let's look at an example of calculating the debt payoff ratio for Coach Inc., the marketer of fine accessories and gifts for women and men. In June 2008, Coach reported an annual profit of $783 million. It also reported that it had long-term debt of $2.6 million. Using the formula to calculate Coach's debt payoff ratio would look like this:

$$\frac{\$2.6 \text{ million}}{\$783 \text{ million}} = 0.003 \text{ Debt Payoff in Time}$$

The resulting answer will provide the investor with the debt payoff in days, months or years or a combination of those periods. For example, if you arrive at a number such as 2.5 when calculating the debt payoff, it means that it will take two-and-a-half years to pay off the long-term debt out of a company's current annual profit. Looking at Coach Inc., we find that it has a debt payoff ratio of 0.003, which means that it is capable of paying off its long-term debt in less than one day. It also has a debt-to-equity ratio of 0.02. The results of these two ratios prove that Coach is a financially strong company that carries almost no long-term debt.

STEP TWO. The business must have consistent annual increases in its earnings per share (EPS).

Look at a business's earnings per share for the last seven to 10 years to determine if the earnings have increased consistently. Consistent increases in earnings per share tell us that a business is soundly managed. Look for substantial increases in earnings per share of 15% or more annually because as earnings increase, so should a stock's price. Let's look at the earnings of Coach and the earnings of Chico's FAS Inc. so that you can see exactly what I mean when I talk about a stock having consistent increases in its earnings per share. Let's compare their earnings history for 10 years from 1999 to 2008.

COACH INC. (COH) EARNINGS PER SHARE 1999-2008

YEAR	1999	2000	2001	2002	2003	2004	2005	2006	2007	2008
EPS	0.05	0.14	0.19	0.24	0.39	0.62	0.86	1.19	1.69	2.17

CHICO'S FAS INC. (CHS) EARNINGS PER SHARE 1999-2008

YEAR	1999	2000	2001	2002	2003	2004	2005	2006	2007	2008
EPS	0.10	0.17	0.25	0.39	0.57	0.78	1.06	0.98	0.52	-0.11

First, I would like to note both companies have been excellent investment choices in the past, but when comparing them at this moment, it's very clear that Coach has what is considered to be a perfect earnings history. Its performance has been impressive, and it would be an excellent holding when purchased at the right price. Businesses with consistent earnings like those of Coach are the types that I want to own. Chico's FAS is a very good company that has made many investors a lot of money in the past and may do so in the future, but its earnings are not consistently increasing as they once did, which makes it hard for investors like me to place a value on a share of its stock. If I'm able to value a stock with confidence, I would be more inclined to purchase it if the price is right, even if its earnings are not as consistent as those of Coach. In general, I recommend that you stick with companies that have a history of consistent increases in earnings like those of Coach Inc. That's what I try to do. It is stocks like those that will more than likely make you a lot of money over the long term, and I believe that making a lot of money is the ultimate goal of anyone that invests. Notice that I mentioned several times the importance of the stock's price being right and will discuss how I value stocks later on in this book.

STEP THREE. Management must wisely use retained earnings to increase shareholders' equity.

When a business earns a profit, it can do several things with that profit. It can pay the profits to the shareholders in the form of dividends, buy back shares of its common stock, reinvest the profits back into the business, pay off debt, or it can perform a combination of the actions mentioned and perhaps a few others not mentioned. I'm only interested in businesses that produce high rates of earnings growth through the reinvestment of its retained earnings. To that end, I need to know the business's return on retained earnings, or RORE. In other words, I need to know the rate that earnings have increased through the use of retained earnings.

The formula for calculating the return on retained earnings is as follows:

(Earnings Increase) / (Total Earnings – Dividends) = Return on Retained Earnings

Let's look once again at the earnings of Coach to give you a better explanation:

COACH INC. (COH) EARNINGS PER SHARE 1999-2008

YEAR	1999	2000	2001	2002	2003	2004	2005	2006	2007	2008
EPS	0.05	0.14	0.19	0.24	0.39	0.62	0.86	1.19	1.69	2.17

If we were to look at Coach's earnings per share for 1999, we find them to be $0.05 per share. We also find that for 2008, Coach's earned $2.17 per share. This gives us an earnings increase of $2.12. Next, we determine the total earnings by adding up all the yearly earnings from 2000 to 2008. We exclude 1999 from this total because it is the base year. From 2000 to 2008 we had total earnings of $7.49. Since Coach did not pay any dividends during this period, we do not have any dividends to subtract from our total earnings. The calculation would be as follows:

2.17 / 7.49 = 28.9 % Return on Retained Earning

Now, that is an excellent return to achieve on retained earnings. It tells us that Coach's management was very effective at using the shareholders' earnings and reinvesting them back into the business for greater profits. To really get an accurate picture of management's return on retained earnings, the stock needs to have the consistent increase in earnings that I mentioned earlier, and Coach is a very good example of the type of business that I'm talking about.

STEP FOUR. The business must show a five-year history of consistently high returns on equity, also known as the ROE.

A high return on equity is an essential element of top-performing stocks. The return on equity is a gauge of a business's profitability and it also serves as management's report card. The return on equity, like the retained earnings, tells us whether management is effectively using profits to increase shareholders' equity. Favor stocks with an average return on equity of 15% or more.

The return on equity also tells us whether a business has a competitive advantage in its industry and a competitive advantage is to be desired. Let's look at a comparison between the apparel stores Talbots Inc. and Aeropostale Inc. We will look at their returns on equity from 2006 through 2010.

TALBOTS INC. (TLB) RETURNS ON EQUITY 2006-2010

YEAR	2006	2007	2008	2009	2010
ROE	9%	N/A	78%	14%	4%

AEROPOSTALE INC. (ARO) RETURNS ON EQUITY 2006-2010

YEAR	2006	2007	2008	2009	2010
ROE	34%	66%	42%	53%	54%

When looking at Talbots, you will see that its returns on equity have been very inconsistent. In 2007, it apparently did not have a return on equity or its return on equity was negligible. It would be hard for me to place any confidence in the stock's future performance because of its inconsistent history. Also, notice the company only met my 15% minimum requirement in 2008. It's ok if returns on equity are lower than 15% during some time periods, but they should be consistent and average out at 15% or more over the most recent five-year period. When looking at Aeropostale Inc., it consistently had very high returns on equity and if you average out its return on equity for the period shown, you will find that it had a five-year average return on equity of 50%. Now, that's awesome. What's even more impressive is the fact that it had high and consistent returns on equity for the entire 10-year period covered in the report.

STEP FIVE. The business must show a five-year history of consistently high returns on capital, also known as the ROC.

Top performers must have consistently high annual returns on capital. The return on capital lets us see if management is effective in its use of the business's capital. Look to purchase stocks of businesses that are capable of obtaining average annual returns on capital of 15% or more. The return on capital is obtained by taking the net income and dividing it by the total capital that the business invested. Of course, you need not worry about performing this calculation because the returns on capital will already be available for you on many of the financial websites or contained in the stock reports that are provided freely on several websites. Let's look at Talbots and Aeropostale again to compare their returns on capital for the years of 2006 through 2010.

TALBOTS INC. (TLB) RETURNS ON CAPITAL 2006-2010

YEAR	2006	2007	2008	2009	2010
ROC	3%	-19%	-99%	N/A	N/A

AEROPOSTALE INC. (ARO) RETURNS ON CAPITAL 2006-2010

YEAR	2006	2007	2008	2009	2010
ROC	34%	66%	42%	53%	54%

From the previous example, you can see that Talbots has very poor returns on capital. As a matter of fact, the investment reports that I obtained the information from had no returns for 2009 and 2010 shown on them. There are clearly some problems going on with Talbots and it's always best to steer clear of stocks of businesses with what appears to be some serious problems. Looking at Aeropostale, it again proved to be a fantastic company with a top-notch management team at the time. Its returns or capital were consistent and high. Like its returns on equity, its returns on capital far exceeded what is average or normal for about any stock from any industry.

STEP SIX. The book value must be consistently increasing at reasonable rates annually. Book value is the common shareholders' net worth divided by the number of shares outstanding.

Although a stock's price may fluctuate wildly from day to day, its book value will remain fairly constant. Increases in book value over time should lead to increases in a stock's price since it tends to impact a stock's price in a similar manner to earnings. Book value is a very important measure and if a business's book value is not growing consistently, it should not be bought. When I speak of reasonable rates, I'm talking about a minimum of 15% annually over the long term, meaning the last seven to 10 years. Of course, very large companies or corporations will probably be unable to obtain growth rates of this magnitude. Just make sure that their book value is increasing consistently. We know from earlier figures that Coach Inc. seems to be the perfect stock, but it's very important that you perform a complete and thorough analysis of any stock of interest to you to determine if it's worthy of being called a worry-free investment. You already have seen some examples of what consistency should look like when it's applied to investing, so let's look again at Coach's growth in book value. We will look at its book value from 1999 through 2008 to see if it consistently grew at reasonable yearly rates.

COACH INC. (COH) BOOK VALUE 1999-2008

YEAR	1999	2000	2001	2002	2003	2004	2005	2006	2007	2008
EPS	0.60	0.63	0.42	0.73	1.17	2.06	2.79	3.21	5.13	4.50

As you can see from the numbers, Coach has been consistently growing its book value. Although book value decreased in 2001 and 2008, I would consider those instances minor setbacks. Using my business calculator, I find that Coach has managed to grow its book value by at least 25% annually for the last nine years in the previous example. There are several circumstances that can cause a business's book value to decrease. Dividend payments, issuance of new shares, depreciating assets, or investment losses are just a few situations in which book value could decrease. Keep matters simple by making sure that you only invest in those businesses that are consistently increasing their book value.

STEP SEVEN. The net profit margins of the business must be consistent or increasing.

The net profit margin is an important profitability ratio that tells us the percentage of net profits that each dollar in sales generates. It compares net income with net sales. A business that is well managed should have consistent or increasing net profit margins. Solid net profit margins are usually an indication that a business also has a competitive advantage in its industry.

Let's look at the net profit margins of Talbots and Aeropostale from 2001 through 2010.

TALBOTS INC. (TLB) NET PROFIT MARGINS 2001-2010

YEAR	2001	2002	2003	2004	2005	2006	2007	2008	2009	2010
EPS	8.0	8.0	7.0	6.0	5.0	3.0	N/A	-9.0	-2.0	1.0

AEROPOSTALE INC. (ARO) NET PROFIT MARGINS 2001-2010

YEAR	2001	2002	2003	2004	2005	2006	2007	2008	2009	2010
EPS	10.0	6.0	7.0	9.0	7.0	8.0	8.0	8.0	10.0	10.0

When looking at Talbots, you will see that the net profit margins looked OK from 2001 through 2005, but notice that they began to really drop in 2005, and it was all downhill from there. A drop-in net profit margin is usually a warning that something is wrong within the company or business. Frankly speaking, Talbots' profit margins are terrible, and its weakening margins tells us that management has some serious challenges ahead to get the business turned around and back on track. A failure to do so will do serious harm to the business and may just put Talbots at risk of going out of business or being sold cheap to a stronger competitor. During the same period, Aeropostale's profit margins were excellent. Look for consistent or increasing net profit margins like those in the example of Aeropostale from the years of 2001 to 2010 when selecting stocks for your portfolio.

STEP EIGHT. The business must have a positive free cash flow for each year for the most recent three-year period, and the business's operating cash flow must be equal to or greater than its net income for each of those years.

During my many years of investment research, I have found no one more adamant about checking out a business's cash flow and more specifically a business's free cash flow (FCF) than Jim Slater. Although earnings can be easily manipulated, it's much harder for a business to manipulate its cash flow statement. A positive free cash flow is a further confirmation that the business is financially sound, and it also demonstrates management's ability to make money for the business and its investors. I usually obtain the free cash flow results from the annual cash flow statement, also referred to as the annual statement of cash flow that is freely available at several of the financial websites mentioned throughout this book. Let's look at the results of DeVry Inc., a worldwide provider of educational and training services. DeVry easily met the requirement of having a positive free cash flow for every year for the most recent three-year period.

DeVry Inc.	
Year	Free Cash Flow
2010	261 Million
2011	272 Million
2012	148 Million

For the final step, you will simply need to look again at the annual cash flow statement. According to DeVry's annual cash flow statement, DeVry had operating cash flows for each year of the most recent three-year period that were greater than the net incomes during those periods. Remember, what we want in a worry-free stock is a cash flow from operations that is equal to or greater than the business's net income and DeVry also met this final requirement as you can see from the following table.

DeVry Inc.		
Year	Operating Cash Flow	Net Income
2010	392 Million	280 Million
2011	408 Million	330 Million
2012	277 Million	142 Million

For me, these two checks in step eight are very important steps and I try only to invest in businesses that meet both requirements of this final step of the stress test. When I created my Personal Worry-Free Stock Portfolio, I did not use this cash flow check at the time, and very few original stocks in my Traditional IRA were purchased with this step being a part of my buy decision; however, both portfolios have still performed very well. These cash flow checks are the newest addition to the stress test, and I believe that they will help investors further reduce their risk by picking stocks that are more financially sound investments that also possess very attractive free cash flows. These requirements also serve the purpose of letting us know whether the earnings that have been reported are honest or true. Although many of the pros rely on earnings when making various investment decisions, they also know that with a little accounting trickery, earnings can be easily manipulated by a smart accountant or financial officer. There's a fairly good chance that a business that has cash flows from operations that are equal to or greater than its net income, will report earnings that can be trusted, therefore, further reducing an investor's risk.

Using the stress test that has been explained is the method that I now use to determine if a stock qualifies as a worry-free stock that builds great wealth when bought at the right price and it is the result of studying the most effective investment strategies of the stock market pros. Because of my experience as an investor, I will sometimes make exceptions to some of the requirements of the stress test. For instance, I may purchase a stock that does not meet the required 15% minimum average return on equity or return on capital because some very good companies, because of their large size, may be incapable of producing such high rates of return. With such companies, consistency is still very important when it comes to the stress test. The eight steps in the stress test act synergistically to confirm that a business is financially sound with little to no debt, has a durable competitive advantage, and a top-notch management team that is investor oriented. Don't forget to also check the Motley Fool's Caps ratings for those businesses that meet the requirements of the stress test. Also, check out Gurufocus.com to see which great investors have also purchased the stocks of those companies and to get an idea of how much they paid for them. Lastly, please remember that the stocks that were used in the examples were for informational purpose only and things may change with any or all of them in the future. Sometimes bad companies are able to turn themselves around and sometimes good companies turn into bad investments. Always remember that things change a lot quicker than they use to with stocks and with the stock market.

Section update - June 15, 2017: I used Aeropostale Inc. in some of my earlier examples in this book and to say that the business had been very impressive at the time would be an understatement. During my financial analysis in 2011, the business seemed to be almost perfect, however, Aeropostale is now a good example of why investors must not buy-and-forget a stock. In early 2016, Aeropostale Inc. filed for Chapter 11 bankruptcy protection.

"Average investors can become experts in their own field and can pick winning stocks as effectively as Wall Street professionals by doing just a little research. — Peter Lynch

WHAT IS THE MEANING OF "FAIR VALUE"?

Before deciding what to pay for a stock, you will first need to know what a stock is worth. What a stock is worth and what others are willing to pay for a stock are two different things. Simply put, fair *value* is an estimate of what a stock is worth. It's an estimate because if you were to ask 10 different and experienced investors what a specific stock is worth, you would get 10 different answers. An important ingredient to making money with stocks is to buy them for much less than they are worth. To do so, you will need a very good estimate of a stock's fair value.

I have experimented with several different stock valuation methods and have found that they all tend to assign different fair value estimates to the exact same stock being analyzed. This happens and is to be expected because different methods are going to yield different results. It's important that you use a method that works and that actually makes money for you. It should also be a method that has the approval of some investment pros, is used by them, and has been used by them successfully in the past. Remember, we don't need to reinvent the wheel. Why should we not take advantage of the knowledge of these masters at making money in the stock market?

Once a stock's fair value is determined, you should always purchase it at a discount to its fair value. The discount gives the investor a margin of safety and we will talk a little about that in the next section. The greater the discount of the purchase, the greater the opportunity for a larger profit and the lower the risk of losing money because of the margin of safety that exists. If we are able to achieve annual rates of return of 12%-15% or more over the long term, then we are on our way to building some serious wealth through our program of worry-free investing.

"The stock market is filled with individuals who know the price of everything, but the value of nothing." —Phillip Fisher

MARGIN OF SAFETY

Of all that I have learned about investing, a margin of safety has to be the most important ingredient needed to invest successfully in the stock market, yet, it's very easy to implement within any investment plan or program. The margin of safety is defined as the difference between a stock's market price and its fair value. Again and again, as I studied the investment systems and strategies of some of the world's most successful stock market pros, they especially had what I'm about to mention next in common. Every one of them stressed the importance of purchasing a stock only when it was trading at a discount to its fair value or intrinsic value. In other words, every one of them would only buy stocks that contained a margin of safety based on their estimate of a stock's fair value. By the way, I consider fair value and intrinsic value to be the same and I don't differentiate between the two terms.

Since a business's fair value is difficult to estimate with 100% accuracy, you and I should only purchase a stock that trades at a big discount to its estimated fair value. The lower the purchase price of a stock relative to its fair value, the safer the investment becomes. In my use of a margin of safety, I look to invest in businesses whose stocks are trading at a minimum discount of 25% to my estimate of their fair value and the bigger the discount, the more I like the stock. For example, if I estimate that a specific stock has a fair value of $12 per share, I will only purchase that stock when it can be bought for $9 or less per share in the market.

Throughout my research, I have found margin of safety recommendations of anywhere from 10-50% but I would recommend that you only buy a stock when it can be purchased at a 25% or more discount to your estimate of its fair value. Remember, the bigger the discount, the sweeter the deal gets. When it comes to investing, a margin of safety is important whether you are investing in stocks, bonds, real estate, commodities, a farm, a laundromat, or a multitude of other businesses. With them all, a margin of safety should be considered before one penny is spent. It's got to be there if you are ever going to build great wealth through investing.

"A margin of safety gives you an edge over just blindly buying stocks or an index fund." —Christopher Brown

USING THE MODIFIED PEG RATIO TO FIND BARGAIN PRICED STOCKS

We will look at my primary and favorite method of valuing individual stocks, and it is the PEG ratio. I love the PEG ratio because it's simple to use, very precise, and allows me to quickly identify an undervalued stock. Jim Slater of the United Kingdom, an investment genius, is the creator of the PEG ratio. Peter Lynch and his management team greatly relied on the PEG ratio to help them pick undervalued stocks while he was at the helm of the Magellan Fund where he racked up an impressive compounded rate of return of 29.2% annually for 13 years. A feat that is virtually unheard of in the investment world. What's even more amazing is that he accomplished this feat with a portfolio that contained thousands of stocks. Slater and Lynch are considered to be two of the world's greatest stock market pros by many experts in the investment community. Do you think that's a coincidence?

There are a few drawbacks to using the PEG ratio just as there are with any of the stock valuation methods in use today. I will talk a little about two drawbacks that I think are of the utmost importance to any investor using the PEG ratio. The first is that the PEG ratio has proven to be unreliable when used to value large, mature companies and tends to punish those companies by assigning them values that are too low. Jim Slater states in his book, *Beyond the Zulu Principle,* that some of the best bargains are shares growing 25% annually and trading on a prospective P/E of 15. The term "prospective P/E" that's used by Slater here is commonly referred to as the forward P/E here in the United States. So, the terms can be used interchangeably because they mean the same thing. In the same book, he also states that the PEG ratio should only be applied to growth stocks. The other drawback is that the PEG ratio is limited by its focus on earnings growth. When Slater created the PEG ratio, it was never meant to be used alone, but to be used as an important tool during the fundamental analysis of a stock. It would be a mistake for any investor to buy a stock based solely on its earnings and earnings growth rate. So, in addition to a low PEG ratio, a stock must also pass the stress test explained earlier in this book before it can qualify as one worthy of our purchase. Shortly, I will explain how to use the PEG ratio to value a stock. Lynch's method of using the PEG ratio is slightly different from the manner in which Slater used it, but the end results are the same and those results are the identifying of undervalued stocks and determining what to pay for them. I apply the PEG ratio in the same manner that Lynch does because it actually places a monetary value on the stock being valued. It's the method that will be explained to you, but it's still basically the same PEG ratio that was created and used by Slater to find undervalued stocks. Slater referred to those undervalued stocks as "hidden gems." He defines the PEG ratio (Price/Earnings to Growth) as the relationship between the P/E ratio and its expected rate of earnings per share growth. The PEG ratio is calculated by dividing the prospective P/E of a stock by its estimated earnings growth rate, as demonstrated in the equation below:

$$\text{PEG Ratio} = \frac{\text{Price / Earnings}}{\text{Annual EPS Growth}}$$

Using this ratio, Slater believes that a fairly valued stock would trade at a PEG ratio of 1. Anything above 1 suggests that a stock is overvalued and anything below 1 indicates that a stock is undervalued. Basically, this means that any stock trading at a P/E equal to its estimated earnings growth rate should be considered fairly valued and any stock trading at a P/E lower than its estimated earnings growth rate should be considered undervalued. The manner in which Slater calculates a stock's PEG ratio results in a numerical value being assigned to that stock. For example, let's say that you have a stock that has a prospective P/E of 15 that will grow its EPS by 30% over the next 5 years. He would take the P/E of 15 and divide it by 30, which is the EPS growth rate. The result of the calculation is 0.50 also known as the PEG by

Slater. Since the resulting number is much lower than 1, then a stock with this particular PEG ratio would be considered extremely undervalued. As mentioned earlier, I use the PEG ratio in the same manner that Lynch does. So, let's take a look at it in action. Since the P/E ratio of any company that's fairly valued equals its growth rate, I replace the P/E ratio with the estimated earnings growth rate, and then I multiply the stock's estimated earnings per share by the estimated earnings growth rate. The following equation demonstrates exactly what I'm talking about. Using the original PEG ratio to calculate a stock's fair value will give you the exact same result as this modified version of the PEG ratio.

(Next Year's Estimated EPS) X (Estimated Earnings Growth Rate)
= Stock's Fair Value

Let's look at an example of how the original PEG ratio works, and then we will look at how the modified version serves the same purpose. Looking at a 2010 stock report for Aeropostale, a mall-based retailer that targets its clothing and accessories to teenagers, we find earnings were expected to grow at an annual rate of 14% for the next five years. Analysts also estimated that Aeropostale would earn $2.82 per share in 2011. Since the original PEG ratio states that a fairly valued stock should trade at a P/E ratio that's equal to its growth rate, this means that Aeropostale trading at a P/E of 14 would be considered a fairly valued stock. Estimated earnings for next year are $2.82 per share. Multiplying those earnings by the P/E of 14 gives us a fair value of $39.48 per share using the original PEG ratio. Using the modified PEG ratio, next year's earnings for Aeropostale are $2.82 per share and Aeropostale's earnings are expected to grow by 14% annually for the next five years. Take the $2.82 earnings estimate and multiply it by the estimated growth rate, which gives a fair value of $39.48 per share. Of course, your goal should never be to purchase a fairly valued stock, but to purchase an undervalued one. Jim Slater has said the brokers' consensus estimates are the most reliable estimates of future earnings and performs his PEG calculations on a rolling 12-month basis. There has been much debate concerning what time period to use when estimating the annual growth rate of stocks. You will usually find recommendations of one-year forward earnings growth estimates to five-year earnings growth estimates. I prefer to use the five-year earnings growth estimates because I'm a long-term investor, and I believe that five-year growth estimates provide a cushion for stock market volatility. I perform my own estimates and they are not as conservative as the brokers' consensus estimates or analysts' estimates, but only the analysts' consensus estimates were used in this book. Since their earnings estimates are more conservative than mine, you will pay less for a stock, not more, which equals a greater profit for you, and that's a good thing.

Remember, Morningstar.com, Zacks.com, Money.msn.com, Finance.yahoo.com and Fool.com are some of my favorite sites to use for my research. Of course, you will only need to refer to one or two websites to obtain all the information that you will need to perform your stock analysis. Next, I'm going to give you a few more examples of how to value a stock using the PEG ratio. Every stock that is reviewed has already met the requirements of the stress test that was presented earlier.

First, we will look at Almost Family Inc. Almost Family is a provider of home health services and operates in several states. Almost Family receives income for its services from federal, state, public and private sources. Looking at Almost Family's 2010 stock report, we find that Almost Family traded at $27.58 per share at that time. Earnings have grown at a rate of 52% annually for the last 5 years and are expected to grow at a rate of 15% annually for the next five years. Analysts also estimate that Almost Family will earn $2.99 per share next year. Using the modified version of the PEG Ratio, the calculation would be as follows:

$$\$2.99 \text{ (2011 EPS Estimate) X 15 (5 Year Earnings Growth Rate Estimate)}$$
$$= \$44.85 \text{ (Fair Value)}$$

At this point, I discount the fair value that I arrive at by 25%, meaning that I would look to buy Almost Family for about $33.64 per share or less. Of course, the lower the price, the more excited I get. This gives me the margin of safety that Benjamin Graham and Jim Slater have so often stressed in their writings and at the same time sets me up for those exceptional returns that I hope to receive from buying the stock at a discount. Almost Family is clearly a buy at its current trading price of $27.58.

$44.85 (Fair Value) X .75 (discount multiple) = $33.64 (Purchase Price)

Let's take a look at Coach. Coach is well known for its line of fine handbags, but also sells watches, jewelry, fragrance, shoes, clothing, and other items. Coach has had a very impressive run by managing to grow its earnings above 40% annually for more than 10 years. Although growth has slowed, it's still an excellent stock when purchased at the right price. Looking at Coach's 2010 stock report, we find that Coach was trading at $41.19 per share.

Coach had also managed to maintain an earnings growth rate of 18% for the previous five years, and analysts estimated Coach would grow its earnings at 14% annually for the next five years. Analysts also estimated earnings of $2.65 per share for 2011.

$2.65 (2011 EPS Estimate) X 14 (5 Year Earnings Growth Rate Estimate)
= $37.10 (Fair Value)
$37.10 (Fair Value) X .75 (Discount Multiple) = $27.83 (Purchase Price)

I would not buy it at a trading price of $41.19 because I'm looking for that margin of safety that comes with buying it at the discounted price of $27.83. However, Coach is one stock worth watching.

Let's next see if Joy Global Inc. is a buy at its 2010 price of $66.44 per share. Joy Global is a manufacturer and servicer of a variety of mining equipment used in the mining industry. Their equipment and services are used in the mining of the various types of metals, coal and oil sands. Referring to a 2010 stock report, we find that Joy Global had managed to grow its earnings at an annual rate of 43% for the previous five years, and analysts estimated it would continue to grow its earnings at an annual rate of 13% for the following five years. Analysts also estimated earnings would be $4.16 per share for 2011.

$4.16 (2011 EPS Estimate) X 13 (5 Year Earnings Growth Rate Estimate)
= $54.08 (Fair Value)
$54.08 (Fair Value) X .75 (Discount Multiple) = $40.56 (Purchase Price)

As you can see, Joy Global was an overvalued stock at the trading price of $66.44. One very important quality that every great investor must possess is patience. A stock that is too expensive right now will usually find your price range sooner or later. Most of the time it happens faster than you would expect.

Finally, we will look at DeVry. You have probably seen those nicely produced commercials about DeVry that promote their institutions and training programs. DeVry has been a very impressive business that seems to be doing everything right. DeVry earnings have grown 43% annually for the last five years. Management has shown that it is efficient and effective with high returns on equity and high returns on capital over the last 10 years. Looking at DeVry's 2010 stock report, we find it was trading at $38.44 per share at that time. Analysts expected earnings to grow at 19% annually over the following five years, and estimated DeVry would earn $4.61 per share in 2011.

$4.61 (2011 EPS Estimate) x 19 (5 Year Earnings Growth Rate Estimate)
= $87.59 (Fair Value)
$87.59 (Fair Value) X .75 (Discount Multiple) = $65.69 (Purchase Price)

Using the PEG ratio, we can clearly see that DeVry was a seriously undervalued stock. We could literally discount the fair value by 50% and it would still be a buy and in my opinion, a very strong buy.

If you are interested in learning more about the PEG ratio or using it in the same manner that Jim Slater uses it, I recommend that you read *The Zulu Principle* and *Beyond the Zulu Principle*, two excellent books written by the man himself. I actually created a practice portfolio and picked eight stocks for it using the PEG ratio in the same manner that Slater does, and in about six months the portfolio had about a 40% gain, which is very impressive. All stocks in that practice portfolio were required to have PEG ratios of 0.60 or less.

The extraordinary success that Slater and Lynch have achieved through their use of the PEG ratio, along with their investment programs, proves that it is a very effective tool when used to identify and to value stocks. I believe that the small investor can achieve phenomenal results through its use. For other stock valuing methods, I recommend that investors check out GuruFocus's tutorial, "How to Value Stocks." The tutorial, which explains a variety of methods for valuing stocks, can be found at GuruFocus.com and on Youtube.com. I am almost certain that most serious investors will find the information very useful and very educational. Lastly, I will leave you with a bit of wisdom from Benjamin Graham. Graham said that if you are not certain if a stock is worth its selling price, wait until it has fallen lower in price before purchasing it.

"Businesses don't change in value as quickly as the market." —*Mario Gabelli*

USING THE P/E RATIO TO ESTIMATE
A SHARE'S TRADING PRICE

Although I have already explained the primary method that I use to determine a stock's fair value, any subject on how to value a stock would be incomplete without a discussion of using the P/E ratio to place some value or price on a stock. I mentioned earlier that what a stock is worth and what others are willing to pay for it are two different things. It's my belief that the P/E ratio, when used alone, is a poor measure to use to determine a stock's fair or intrinsic value. On the other hand, I think that the P/E ratio is an excellent tool to use when attempting to determine what others are willing to pay for a particular stock. In other words, it's a great tool for estimating what a stock's trading price should be based on its past trading history. Many stock market pros rely on the P/E ratio as an important and vital investment tool and have achieved amazing success through its use. Although I never rely solely on the P/E ratio when estimating a stock's value, I still find the P/E ratio to be a very useful measure when deciding if a stock is overvalued or undervalued, expensive or cheap relative to the stock market as a whole and relative to other stocks within the same industry or sector.

When using the P/E ratio to estimate a stock's trading price, I believe that the P/E ratio is especially helpful for use with very large companies that are no longer capable of growing very fast anymore. Although I favor investing in businesses that are capable of growing their EPS at an annual rate of 15% or more, I know that many excellent companies may be incapable of such growth because of their vast size, slowing revenue growth, and shrinking market share. Companies such as General Electric, Nike, Proctor & Gamble, Wal-Mart and Coca-Cola are huge businesses that are highly unlikely to be able to grow their revenue and EPS at the higher rates they were capable of when they were much younger and smaller companies; yet, these are still excellent businesses to invest in when their prices are right. Because of the size and slower growth rate of these companies, the PEG ratio along with some other valuing methods sometimes assign valuations that are too low for such wonderful, safe and consistently performing businesses, and that's where the P/E ratio can be an effective remedy. Of course, the P/E ratio is also effective to use with small to mid-sized companies too.

When using the P/E ratio, you should use the long-term average annual P/E ratio for better and more accurate estimates of a stock's trading price. Remember, when we use the P/E ratio in the manner that's being taught here, we are not determining a stock's fair or intrinsic value, but we are seeing what investors were willing to pay for the stock in the past based on its EPS estimates and we are estimating the price they are likely to pay now or at some point in the future for a specific stock. Anytime the term "long-term" is used throughout this book, it's referring to a period of seven to 10 years. When referring to P/E ratios, if only a five-year history is available, I will use it but never less than five years for my estimates. Now, let's take a look at a few examples of how to use the P/E ratio to estimate a stock's trading price.

We will look first at Bed Bath & Beyond, a supplier of home furnishings, bed linens and other brand name merchandise to the public. The following table shows the average annual P/E ratios that Bed Bath & Beyond traded for between 2001 and 2010.

BED BATH & BEYOND (BBBY) AVERAGE ANNUAL P/E RATIO
2001-2010

YEAR	2001	2002	2003	2004	2005	2006	2007	2008	2009	2010
P/E	40.0	33.8	30.5	23.5	20.7	17.5	16.5	16.9	14.7	14.2

We must first determine the total of the P/E averages by adding the values given for all 10 years from 2001 through 2010. Once we have the total, we divide it by 10 to obtain our long-term average annual P/E rate. The equation for Bed Bath & Beyond follows:

228.3 (Sum Of P/E Averages) / 10 (Total Number of Years) = 22.8
(Long-Term Avg. P/E Ratio)

Analysts estimated Bed Bath & Beyond would earn $4.70 in 2011 and the stock traded at $62.85 per share at the time of the report in early 2012. To estimate the stock's trading price using the P/E ratio, you will simply multiply the estimated EPS for 2011 by the long-term average P/E ratio. The equation would be as follows:

$4.70 (2011 EPS Estimate) x 22.8 (Long-Term Average P/E Ratio)
= $107.16 (Estimated Trading Price).

Based on what investors were willing to pay in the past for Bed Bath & Beyond, shares should now have been trading for about $107.16 instead of the $65.85 that the shares traded for at the time, meaning that Bed Bath & Beyond shares were trading for about 39% less than investors have been willing to pay in the past for its shares. We can clearly see that Bed Bath & Beyond was a buy at its trading price of $65.85 per share.

Let's now take a look at FactSet Research Systems Inc. to estimate its trading price from the use of the P/E ratio. Looking at a 2011 stock report for FactSet Research Systems, its average annual P/E ratio history is contained in the following table:

FACTSET RESEARCH SYSTEMS INC. (FDS) AVERAGE ANNUAL P/E RATIO 2002-2011

YEAR	2002	2003	2004	2005	2006	2007	2008	2009	2010	2011
P/E	26.7	22.8	24.6	24.0	26.0	27.4	23.9	16.2	22.2	26.3

When we add the average annual P/E ratios up for the years shown, we find that our sum is 240.1 and we will need to divide the sum by the number of years for which the average annual P/E ratios are supplied, which is 10, to obtain our long-term average P/E ratio. Let's look next at the equation for FactSet Research Systems Inc.

240.1 (Sum Of P/E Averages) / 10 (Total Number of Years) = 24.0
(Long-Term Avg. P/E Ratio)

Analysts estimated FactSet Research Systems would earn $4.30 per share in 2012 and the stock traded at $90.05 per share at the time the report was prepared. To estimate the stock's trading price using the P/E ratio, multiply the 2012 estimated EPS of $4.30 by the long-term average P/E ratio of 24. The equation would be as follows:

$4.30 (2011 EPS Estimate) x 24.0 (Long-Term Average P/E Ratio) = $103.20 (Estimated Trading Price).

Based on what investors were willing to pay in the past for FactSet Research Systems, shares should have been trading for about $103.20 but were trading at $90.05 at the time, which means that FactSet Research Systems shares were trading for about 13% less than investors have been willing to pay for its shares in the past. Even if I use this method to determine my purchase price of a stock, I would still require a margin of safety just as I do with the other methods that I use to perform my stock valuations.

Finally, we will look at Syntel Inc., a provider of information technology and knowledge process outsourcing services. Looking at a 2013 stock report for Syntel Inc., we find the following average annual P/E ratios for the years from 2003 through 2012.

SYNTEL INC. (SYNT) AVERAGE ANNUAL P/E RATIO 2003-2012

YEAR	2003	2004	2005	2006	2007	2008	2009	2010	2011	2012
P/E	21.3	20.3	24.4	17.9	23.6	13.7	11.3	14.7	17.3	12.8

When we add the average annual P/E ratios up for the 10 years shown, we come up with a total of 177.3 and as I demonstrated in previous examples, we need to divide the sum by 10 to come up with our long-term average annual P/E ratio for Syntel Inc. Take a look at the equation for Syntel Inc.

177.3 (Sum Of P/E Averages) / 10 (Total Number of Years) = 17.7
(Long-Term Avg. P/E Ratio)

Analysts estimated that Syntel would earn $4.40 per share in 2013 and the
stock traded at $64.69 per share at the time the report was prepared. To
estimate the trading price for Syntel Inc., we need to multiply the 2013
estimated EPS of $4.40 by the long-term average P/E ratio of 17.7 or 18 if
rounded. The equation would be as follows:

$4.40 (2013 EPS Estimate) x 17.7 (Long-Term Average P/E Ratio) =
$77.88 (Estimated Trading Price).

With Syntel Inc. trading at $64.69 per share compared to an estimated
trading price of $77.88 per share, we find that Syntel Inc. shares were trading
for almost 17% less than investors have been willing to pay for its shares in
the past. As you can see, the P/E ratio and more specifically, the average
annual P/E ratio is a very useful measure for estimating a stock's trading price
and it's simple to use. I like simplicity and hope that you do, too.

*"Great companies bought at great prices should be like great friends — you do not
drop them precipitously." —Shelby M.C. Davis*

THE STOCK SCREENER:
AN INVESTOR'S BEST FRIEND

I must confess I have literally spent thousands of hours researching and studying stocks. The truth is that much of that time could have been put to better use, if only I had known about stock screeners at the time. I now greatly depend on stock screeners when I perform my research and wouldn't want to be without them. A stock screener is a very powerful investment tool that scans a database to search for stocks that meet certain criteria that has been specified by an investor. Stock screeners may be standalone software programs or web-based programs. To date, I have only used the free, web-based programs, and I personally think that they are excellent and many of them are free of charge.

Without the use of stock screeners, searching for stocks that meet the stringent requirements that have been set forth in this book is like searching for a needle in a haystack. Remember, just on the American exchanges alone there are thousands of stocks, and screeners save time by eliminating those that do not meet an investor's requirements. Try searching for stocks that meet the requirements of the stress test explained earlier using any method of your choice except stock screeners, and then perform your research again using a stock screener to see which method is better. When you are finished, I bet that you will conclude that using a stock screener is easily the best method for performing your search. A stock screener will generate a list of stocks that will need to be further studied and is merely the first step in the process of selecting worry-free stocks to build your portfolio. I use three different screeners to perform my searches and any more than two to three good screeners really is not needed. By using at least two screeners, you increase the likelihood of finding several candidates that meet the search criteria that you require. Because each screener is different, the search parameters will vary somewhat, but the final result should be the same. I use the following screeners and all three are currently free of charge:

Motley Fool Caps Screener — caps.fool.com

FINVIZ Screener — finviz.com

Google Stock Screener — google.com/finance/stockscreener

If you refer to the Appendix, you will find that I have provided you with some screening criteria that can be used in your search for stocks based on the investment systems and strategies of specific investment pros. Once you have run at least two stock screeners, you will, without a doubt, generate a large number of stocks that require additional research. To quickly weed out those stocks that clearly do not belong on your list, look at the seven to 10-year earnings history of each stock. If the stock does not have at least seven years of earnings, disqualify it without exception. Does the stock have at least seven years of consistent earnings with earnings increasing each year? If not, eliminate the stock from further research. I will usually make minor exceptions to this rule by allowing for one year of losses, as long as the rest of the earnings pattern looks good. If earnings are OK, look next at debt. Take the stock's total long-term debt for its most recent full year and divide the long-term debt by the stock's total net income for its most recent full year. If the resulting number is greater than five, eliminate the stock. Performing this analysis is quick and will probably disqualify at least 90% of the stocks that have been retrieved by the stock screeners, but will leave you with stocks that have the best opportunities of being the right ones that put you on the right path to building wealth. You will also save yourself a ton of time using this screening process. That is if time could be physically weighed. Again, remember that the stocks retrieved by a screener or screening tool should not be considered a buy list, but a thorough financial analysis should be performed on each stock before determining whether or not to purchase them.

"To become a successful investor, you must be committed to the concept that investing in equities is a proven way to build wealth over generations." — *Christopher C. Davis*

THE PRACTICE PORTFOLIO

When I started investing in stocks, I did not think about creating a practice portfolio to test the effectiveness of what little information I knew about investing. Now in addition to my two real stock portfolios that I manage, I have three practice portfolios (virtual portfolios) that I mostly monitor but have made very few changes to. All three portfolios were created using the principles and strategies set forth within this book. When I talk about a practice portfolio, I am referring to what is known as paper trading or virtual trading. Here's how Investopedia defines paper trading: *Using simulated trading to practice buying and selling securities without actual money being involved. While a paper trade can be done by simply keeping track of hypothetical trading positions, it usually involves the use of a stock market simulator (virtual trading) that has the look and feel of an actual stock market where budding investors can hone their trading skills.*

So, in reality, the practice portfolio that I use and that I would recommend to others allows the investor to buy and sell stocks in real-time with a real account; however, with the practice account, the investor is using fake money. The performance of investments in the practice portfolio is also shown in real-time. There's a saying that "practice makes perfect," and most of us have learned that if an individual wants to be good at performing a particular task or displaying a certain skill at the highest level, he or she must practice it. Unfortunately, when I started investing, I dived into it head first without any knowledge of what I was really doing, and it resulted in me losing most of my savings. To make matters worse, I lost money that I really could not afford to lose, and it left me in a terrible financial predicament. One very important rule of investing is to never invest money in the stock market that you cannot afford to lose. Had I used a practice portfolio when I was day trading, there's no doubt that I would have learned that day trading doesn't work for most people. If you decide that you would like to set up a practice account or some practice accounts, there are many financial and investment websites that offer them for free. So, there's absolutely no reason to pay for such services. Once the account or accounts have been created, use them to test the principles and strategies presented in this book or from other sources that interest you. One thing is for sure: with a practice account, you're not going to lose any real money; but if you give it time, you will be able to draw your own conclusion about what works and what doesn't.

At the time of this writing, each one of my practice portfolios is in the black, meaning that they have made money. Portfolio #1 is up 22.9%, Portfolio #2 is up 62.4%, and Portfolio #3 is up 92.1%. I use the websites howthemarketworks.com and finance.yahoo.com for my practice portfolios. I really like both websites, but I recommend you find and use websites you like when setting up your practice portfolio or portfolios. Finally, it is important to realize the practice portfolio is a tool; and to obtain the greatest benefit from its use, it must be taken seriously. Investopedia put it best by saying that investment decisions should be made based on the same risk-return objectives, investment constraints, and trading horizon as in real life.

"Sometimes buying early on the way down looks like being wrong, but it isn't."
—Seth Klarman

THE BUSINESS CALCULATOR

The business calculator can be a hand-held device or an online program that allows individual investors to perform a variety of investment calculations. The business calculator is a valuable tool that no serious investor should be without, because it's this type of investor that eventually develops the desire to perform his own calculations as his confidence as an investor grows. There are hundreds if not thousands of investment and financial websites that offer online business calculators that can be used free-of-charge. I prefer to use a hand-held calculator instead of the online versions simply because of the convenience of being able to take it with me while on the go. I will usually take several stock reports with me to dental and medical appointments or just about anywhere else where I'm going to be sitting idle for long periods of time. I currently use a Texas Instruments BA II that was purchased at Wal-Mart for around $30. If you choose to purchase a hand-held calculator, do not spend a lot of money on it because an expensive calculator is not needed for the calculations that you will be performing. Personally, I think that the online calculators are fantastic and have found that the only drawback for me is limited access to the internet when I'm away from home. Regardless of which version of the business calculator that you choose to use, get familiar with it and learn to use it to perform at least basic calculations such as rate of return, annual earnings growth rates, present value, and future value. Next, we will look briefly at some explanations of the calculations just mentioned.

Rate of Return - The rate of return is the gain or loss on an investment over a specified period of time that's expressed as a percentage increase or decrease over the initial investment cost. Let me give you an example. If I bought a stock 10 years ago for $15 per share and the stock is currently trading for $90 per share, using a business calculator, I find that I have received an annual compound rate of return of 19.6%. Not a bad return for an investment, when I consider that over the long term most investment experts fail to outperform the stock market as a whole, and the market's average annual returns are much lower than 19.6% over the long term.

Annual Earnings Growth Rate - This rate gives us the compounded rate at which earnings are growing on an annual basis. Knowing how a stock has performed over the previous five-year period and the seven- to 10-year period is essential to making any sort of acceptable prediction of how a stock can be expected to perform in the future. For instance, looking at Atwood Oceanics' 2010 stock report, the annual earnings growth rate for the last five years was 105%. Now, that's an amazing accomplishment that will no doubt diminish over the next five years, but knowing that the business has achieved such phenomenal growth allows me to predict future annual earnings growth estimates on the high side. I can still see Atwood Oceanics achieving an annual earnings growth rate of at least 15% to 30% over the next five years.

Present Value - The present value tells us the current worth of a future sum of money based on a specific rate of return. To put it more simply, present value tells us the amount that a future sum of money is worth today when invested for a specified rate of return. Looking again at Atwood Oceanics, its 2009 earnings per share was $3.89. Let's just say that I believe that it's capable of growing its annual earnings by 30% over the next five years. Of course, my EPS growth estimate may be way off the mark, which would result in the earnings being way off course, too.

Remember, these are just estimates, and my estimates tend to be on the high side compared to those provided by the analysts. Even so, even the analyst estimated an EPS growth rate of 20% over the next five years for Atwood Oceanics. Using my business calculator, it tells me that Atwood Oceanics should earn $14.44 per share at the end of the fifth year if it can grow its EPS at an annual rate of 30% during the next five-year period. Atwood Oceanics has traded at an average annual P/E of 17 for the last five years. Multiplying the estimated earnings for the fifth year of $14.44 by the average annual P/E of 17 would give us an estimated stock price of $245.48 at the end of the fifth year. Now, here is where present value becomes important. Let's say I desire at least a 20% annual compound return on my investment. Using my business calculator, I enter the future value of $245.48. I also enter the period of time, which is the five years that my money will be invested. Last, I enter my desired return of 20% annually and hit the compute button on my calculator. It tells me that I will need to presently buy Atwood Oceanics at $98.65 per share or less to achieve my desired return. The $98.65 is what would be known as the present value.

Future Value - I have given you a very good example of present value and future value is, of course, the opposite of present value. It's something that we are all accustomed to thinking about. When we invest money into something, we all want to know what it's going to be worth in the future, whether it's at the end of five years or five days. With the business calculator, you can perform this calculation as well as the others previously mentioned in a jiffy. The business calculator is an extremely handy tool to have and it's a necessity for those who want to perform their own financial calculations.

Section update: I completed this section of the book several years ago and thought now would be an appropriate time to give you an update concerning Atwood Oceanics Inc. On Jan. 29, 2016, the stock closed at $6.13 per share and had traded at a high of $35.66 within the 52-week period. The stock has taken a terrible beating as well as the entire energy and the commodities sector. In my opinion, stocks within these sectors are trading at recession-like prices with many trading at lows not seen during the Great Recession. For instance, Atwood Oceanics has traded at a high of $59.49 within the last five years and closed at $6.13 per share on Jan. 29, 2016. Atwood Oceanics' poor price performance is a real shocker and further proof that anything can happen with stocks. I own shares in my Traditional IRA, and my average cost is $24.83 per share. My plan is to continue holding my shares because I'm convinced that the market has placed a ridiculously low price on Atwood Oceanics' shares.

"It might not be today or tomorrow, but if you do your homework well, the stock market will eventually recognize the inherent value that attracted you to the bargain opportunity in the first place." —Joel Greenblatt

PART THREE

THE WORRY-FREE STOCK PORTFOLIO

BUILDING YOUR WORRY-FREE
STOCK PORTFOLIO

Most people think that it takes large amounts of time and money to build a great stock portfolio, but that's just not the truth. If you are just getting started, then you probably don't have a lot of money to invest all at once. The truth is that this book was written especially for you. You must simply build your stock portfolio one to two stocks at a time. Meaning, you will purchase shares of a specific stock each time funds are available until you have reached your desired holdings of that stock. Some may say that this method is risky, but I would have to disagree with those individuals. Remember, you and I only want the best performing, worry-free stocks in our stock portfolios. They are stocks that have already proven themselves with a strong, long-term performance history. Risk is greatly reduced when you buy these long-term top performers.

GETTING STARTED

The very first thing you should do to get started is open an online investment account such as an Individual Retirement Account that was described earlier. The online account allows you to place all of your trades from the comfort of your home and allows you to easily monitor your portfolio. There's usually a minimum deposit required to open any sort of investment account regardless of the type with the exception that with the Individual Retirement Account, direct rollovers from other retirement accounts are permitted. The minimum deposit varies with each financial institution and the type of account being established. It will be necessary for you to research several brokerages to find the one that's right for you. Once the account has been established, you should set up direct deposit through your employer if it's available. Direct deposit allows you to have a percentage of your pay or a dollar amount of your pay that you specify deposited into your brokerage account automatically. Use of direct deposit makes saving easy; and with its use, you are actually paying yourself first. <u>Failure of most people to pay themselves first is the main reason many of them find themselves living from paycheck to paycheck, even after many years of working.</u> If you are self-employed or your company does not offer direct deposit, there's still another way to make investing automatic and it's through the use of automatic transfers. Automatic transfers are transfers that your bank will make for you by taking money from an account that you designate and depositing it into another account. Automatic transfers are an excellent way to go if direct deposit is not available for you. Scottrade® offers a service called Money Direct that allows individual investors to transfer funds directly into their Scottrade account from another financial institution such as a bank or credit union. The transactions are performed online and can be completed within a matter of seconds with today's computers. Other discount brokers may offer similar services, but I have been very pleased with Scottrade and the services that it offers.

Next, I recommend that you set a goal to deposit a minimum of $50 per week or $100 biweekly into your brokerage account. Doing so will give you $200-$250 to invest each month. In a year's time, you could actually save as much as $2600. With it, you could easily buy five stocks, putting $500 into each one of them. Of course, if you can save more, do it. I have been investing for many years now and place all of my trades online and have never had any problems. I do recommend that you choose a reputable online broker such as TD Ameritrade®, E*Trade®, Charles Schwab®, or Scottrade®. Every time the cash balance in my brokerage account would hit the $500 mark, I would purchase shares of a worry-free stock as I was building up my portfolio. If you build your portfolio in this manner, you will find yourself with an impressive portfolio in a very short period of time. Building a worry-free stock portfolio like the pros isn't hard unless you want it to be.

"If you buy stocks when they are out of favor and unloved, and sell them into strength when other investors recognize their merits, you'll often go home with handsome gains." —John Neff

KEEP YOUR PORTFOLIO SMALL

Most investors are unsure about how many stocks to hold in their portfolios. Studies have shown that investors that keep their portfolios small improve their chances of beating the market. A worry-free stock portfolio should contain a minimum of 10 and a maximum of about 20 stocks based on my research of the market pros.

According to an article dated Sept. 15, 2000, that I read on *TheStreet.com*, Jim Cramer said he believes the average person can only monitor about six stocks effectively in a portfolio including him. Jim Cramer undoubtedly has a team of money managers helping him, and that's why his charitable trust contains more than six stocks. Jim Slater says the individual investor should hold a minimum of 10 stocks and a maximum of 12 stocks in his portfolio. Robert Hagstrom, author of *The Warren Buffett Portfolio,* has performed extensive research into portfolio management. As he states in *The Warren Buffett Portfolio*, "Your probability of beating the market goes up as the size of your portfolio goes down. With a 15-stock portfolio, you have a 1-in-4 chance of beating the market. With a 250-stock portfolio, your chances are 1 in 50." Out of curiosity, I decided to do some research into the number of stocks contained in the portfolios of some of America's top money managers. I was only interested in those that had managed to obtain long-term returns above 15% and the results of my research are contained in the table that follows. The information was obtained several years ago and there's no doubt it's no longer accurate, but we definitely can learn something from it. Looking at result of the table, we find that the long-term average annual rate of return for the portfolios listed is 23.3%, and the average numbers of stocks in these winning portfolios are twelve when we exclude famed investor Robert Rodriquez who did an amazing job with a portfolio containing a much larger number of stocks than the average of 12 found in the portfolios of the other great investors used in the comparison.

INVESTOR'S NAME	STOCKS HELD	LONG -TERM PERFORMANCE
Ian Cumming	5	33% annually from 1978-2004
Glenn Greenberg	12	23% annually from 1984-2004
Robert Karr	9	22% annually from 1996-2010
Seth Klarman	17	20% annually from inception in 1983
Edward Lampert	11	29% annually from 1988-2009
Mohnish Pabrai	17	29% annually from 1999-2006
David Swenson	10	17% annually for last ten years based on the date of the article.
Robert Rodriquez	25-45	17% annually from 1984-2007
Lou Simpson	13	20% annually from 1980-2004

It's pretty hard to argue against the results that these portfolios have achieved although most are concentrated in the number of stocks that they contain. Dave Kansas, former editor-in-chief of *TheStreet.com,* once said, "For most people, the ability to follow more than a dozen stocks is likely limited. A portfolio of a dozen or so stocks should provide you with the protection of diversification and the focus to build wealth." Isn't it amazing that we have been conditioned to believe that more is better? As you can see, when it comes to investing in stocks, more is detrimental instead of beneficial to a portfolio's performance. So, in reality, less is more when investing in individual stocks. Jordan L. Kimmel, a leading investment expert and successful money manager, states in his book *Magnet Investing,* "It only requires a handful of long-term profits in outstanding companies to create personal independent wealth." In other words, he is saying that it only takes owning stock shares in a few outstanding companies over the long term to become very wealthy.

Remember, if you don't already have the funds to invest, you will have to gradually work your way up to the 10 stocks minimum. By following these recommendations, an investor ends up with a portfolio that allows for good diversification and at the same time, the portfolio is not so large that the investor has a hard time monitoring the stocks. I try to limit my holdings in my own stock portfolios to 20 stocks, but I will sometimes hold more stocks in the portfolios but usually not for very long periods of time. Shortly, I will reveal my portfolios to you. It's my hope that by doing so, you will gain a better understanding of how to create your own portfolio that has good diversification and an excellent selection of undervalued stocks in it. Since your portfolio will be concentrated in number, pick only the best stocks available at your time of purchase and be sure to purchase them with a margin of safety.

"You have to know when you're wrong. Then you sell. Most stocks that I buy are a mistake." —Peter Lynch

WHEN TO SELL A STOCK

Determining when to sell a stock is a decision that even the world's best investors wrestle with. Warren Buffett has said that his holding period for a stock is forever. Does Buffett really hold every stock that he buys forever? Of course not! The point that he is making is that you should always purchase a stock with the intention of holding it forever; therefore, make sure your money has been put into your best investment ideas. Author Robert Hagstrom has written several excellent books about Warren Buffett and his investment strategies. In *The Warren Buffett Portfolio*, he says that an investor should leave his or her portfolio intact for at least five years, as long as the fundamentals for which a particular stock was purchased do not deteriorate. He also says investors should pay no attention to a stock's price volatility because it is a normal part of the investment cycle. In their book *Million Dollar Portfolio*, the Motley Fool team says investors' minimum holding period for each stock that is purchased should be three to five years. As a long-term investor, there will be times when it makes sense to sell or reduce your position in a stock earlier than you had planned. Next, we will talk about different circumstances in which you should consider selling a stock or reducing your position in a stock.

The Time Frame - If you will need the money within five years, it should not be invested in stocks. It would be best to invest your money in safe and stable short-term instruments. Money market accounts, money market funds, and short-term certificates of deposits would be better options. Since the Great Recession struck, some investment professionals now recommend that you not invest any money in stocks that will be needed within 10 years.

An Overvalued Stock - When a stock is significantly overvalued, sell it. Take the proceeds from the sale and invest them into other undervalued stocks that you have researched. The P/E ratio is still one of the best indicators

116

of value. For example, if a stock has traded at an average P/E of 15 for the last seven to 10 years and the business is thriving, but the stock currently trades at a P/E of 30 or more on consistent or increasing EPS, you should seriously consider selling the stock. The PEG ratio is also a very effective method for determining if a stock is now overvalued. I must admit I'm slow to sell an overvalued stock if it's not extremely overvalued because excellent investment choices are hard to find and if they are in my portfolio, it's because I consider them to be excellent selections. When a stock is overvalued by 50%, I would not hesitate to sell it quickly in order to put my money into other investments that are a better value.

Too Much Debt - Too much debt is dangerous for any business because there's always the chance that a business may be unable to pay its debt. Too much debt also puts a business at greater risk of failure if a downturn in the industry or economy were to occur. Upon entering the 2007 recession, thousands of businesses here in the United States literally disappeared overnight and that was before things really got bad. I'm willing to bet that those businesses that were carrying too much debt were the first to go.

Too Much Risk - You have already learned the importance of staying away from investments that are too risky. Sometimes new management will come to a business and begin to implement new policies; along with that implementation they will knowingly or unknowingly expose a business to greater risk. If you purchased the stock of a business that stayed away from very risky practices, but the business has now begun to display risky behaviors that make you uncomfortable, sell the stock and find yourself a better investment.

Loss of Competitive Advantage - You have also learned that we should only be purchasing the stocks of businesses that have a durable competitive advantage. When a business changes its business model, resulting in it losing its competitive advantage, sell the stock. Having a durable competitive advantage is essential to any stock that you and I purchase if we are truly going to invest like the pros do.

The Portfolio Lacks Balance or Diversification - It's very easy for your best performing stock to become the largest holding in your portfolio, and there's absolutely nothing wrong with that. The problem arises when the stock makes up more than 20-25% of your portfolio's total value. I would be very uncomfortable having more than 25% of my portfolio's value tied to just one stock. Legendary investor, Jim Slater suggests that individual investors limit the number of funds invested in a single stock within their portfolios to a maximum of 15%. When your portfolio becomes heavily weighted in one stock, consider reducing your position of that stock to bring more balance and better diversification into your portfolio.

Stock Reaches Its Fair Value – Our goal as investors should always be to purchase a stock at a discount to its fair value and I recommend at least a 25% discount to its fair value. By doing so, when you sell a stock that has reached its fair value, you are guaranteed a gain of at least 25% from the sell. This is a disciplined approach to selling a stock. According to research, it was common for Benjamin Graham to sell a stock once it had a 50% gain in price. If the future prospects of a particular stock looks good, you may decide to sell only a portion of the stock such as half of its shares and hold on to the rest when using this approach.

When Your Analysis is Found to Be Flawed- There will be times when an investor will be very detailed and careful in his or her analysis of a particular company or its stock, only to find out later that his or her analysis is incorrect or flawed. Whether a stock should be sold at that time depends on the seriousness of the error and its impact on the long-term performance of the business. So, when you find that you have incorrectly analyzed a particular business, it is essential for you to take a serious look at all available information to determine whether or not to sell the stock or to continue holding it. One thing is certain, as an investor, you will not always be right when analyzing a company or its stock.

Based on my observation and research, I have not discovered a clear-cut way to determine the optimal time to sell a stock. There will be times that you will sell a stock because it has not performed well, only to see it skyrocket and double or triple in price soon after you sell it. There will also be occasions when you have purchased what seems to be the perfect stock, only to watch it tumble in price and for no apparent reason. Learn what you can from these events and move on. Even Peter Lynch, Jim Slater and other great investors have sold stocks too early or too late. It's going to happen sometimes.

"If the job has been correctly done when a common stock is purchased, the time to sell it is — almost never." —Philip A. Fisher

MONITORING YOUR STOCK PORTFOLIO

A big mistake that many investors make is to monitor the price movement of the stocks in their portfolios on a daily basis. It's quite ridiculous to monitor stocks in such a manner since a stock's price will fluctuate from day to day and sometimes wildly. Those investors that watch their investments daily have adopted the wrong investment plan or approach, and they are likely to stress themselves out when their stocks fall in price. One final time, I will remind you that you must invest for the long-term to really invest like a stock market pro. The stock market is not the place to be if you have a get-rich-quick mentality.

Soon, I'm going to reveal to you both of my stock portfolios. It's my intention to still own every stock in them several years from now although that's highly unlikely to happen. Note, I said, "it's my intention," because that's the mindset I have, and it should be the same mindset you have every time you purchase a stock. Since I'm investing for the long-term, why should I concern myself with the daily gyrations of the stock market or the fluctuations in the prices of my stocks? Please realize that I may need to sell sooner for some unforeseen reason, such as in the cases of Ceradyne Technologies and Questor Pharmaceuticals, or if much better opportunities present themselves, but it's still my intention to hold every stock for the long-term.

We should be able to manage our portfolios more effectively and efficiently by limiting the portfolios to about 20 stocks. Your biggest responsibility as a manager is to stay abreast of what's going on with the businesses of every stock in your portfolio. In other words, keep up with the latest news on every stock. If something of importance has happened, it will make the news. I recommend that about once a month or every few weeks if once a month seems just too long for you, that you go to one or more of the financial websites such as the Motley Fool, Yahoo! Finance, Morningstar, MarketWatch, Seeking Alpha, GuruFocus, or Zacks Investment Research to get the most recent news on your investments. This portfolio checkup should be short and sweet and should take no more than an hour or so to perform. During this check, you are looking to see if anything has happened that would result in you being uncomfortable with continuing to hold any of the stocks in your portfolio. Earlier, I gave you some criteria for when to sell a stock. It's during this monitoring process that every stock in your portfolio should be analyzed using those criteria to determine if any stocks merit selling. If a sell is in order, sell the stock and move on to something better. Just be sure you are not prematurely selling a great stock. Of course, if everything looks good, no further action would be needed.

Following these recommendations would require you to check your portfolio maybe 12-20 times each year, and they are meant to allow you to really be worry-free about your investments. If you stick with these recommendations, I believe you will be a much happier investor while on your path to building wealth.

"If you do your work properly in the beginning, there's really no need to re-analyze a company every 10 minutes." —Charles Royce

MY PERSONAL WORRY-FREE STOCK PORTFOLIO (SEPT. 2008 TO AUG. 2013)

My Personal Worry-Free Stock Portfolio is the first real money portfolio I created for myself based on the principles and strategies set forth in this book. I have learned much since and from the creation of this portfolio and that new information has been included in this book. It has been my intention over the long term to limit the portfolio to a maximum of fifteen stocks from a variety of industries or sectors and to only sell a stock out of the portfolio as a last resort. In other words, I wanted the portfolio to be as passively managed as possible by me even if its performance suffered as a result. By doing so, I strongly believed that it would teach me much over the long term.

I only had a few thousand dollars available to start my investment program and would have had more money to start if I had not lost the $12,000 day-trading. You can start your investment program with a lot less, so don't worry if you don't have much money to get started. To come up with the additional funds that I used to build the portfolio, I got a part-time job. It's not that I needed a part-time job to start my investment program, but I used the income from the work to speed the process along. I also applied several of the money savings strategies listed in the section entitled, "Finding Extra Money to Fund Your Investment Program." Because of the additional income, I was usually able to purchase a decent number of shares of a stock on a weekly or bi-weekly basis, gradually building the portfolio one stock position at a time. Of course, there were times in which I was able to build or add to positions in two or more stocks at the same time. My ability to do so greatly depended on how much money I had available for investing at the time.

The very first purchase for the portfolio was made on Sept. 15, 2008, and the last purchase was completed on March 3, 2010 — meaning all original stock purchases were completed for the portfolio in about a year and a half. Although I'm a believer in long-term investing, I realize that changes in the holdings of the portfolio may have to occur at some point from situations such as mergers, acquisitions, or even bankruptcies. So, even if changes are made to this portfolio, it's my intention to continue to monitor the total return performance of the portfolio so that you can be provided with its up-to-date performance. Next, I'm going to provide you with my Personal Worry-Free Stock Portfolio along with the total returns (gains or losses) and the annual rate of return for each stock contained in the portfolio.

STOCK NAME	STOCK SYMBOL	INITIAL PURCHASE	AVG. COST PER SHARE	LATEST PRICE	GAIN/ LOSS	ANNUAL RETURN
COACH INC.	COH	1-06-2009	$20.38	$53.87	167.5%	23.9%
CERADYNE TECHNOLOGY	CRDN	10-24-2008	$23.60	$35.00	35.2%	SOLD 11/28/12 10.0%
COGNIZANT TECHNOLOGY	CTSH	9-15-2008	$21.86	$72.89	233.4%	27.9%
COVENTRY HEALTH CARE	CVH	5-28-2009	$19.54	$49.99	157.2%	SOLD 5/06/13 26.6%
DXP ENTERPRISES	DXPE	6-02-2009	$14.00	$68.77	391.1%	46.3%
ENGLOBAL INC.	ENG	7-15-2009	$4.63	$1.05	-77.3%	-30.6%
CORPORATE EXECUTIVE	EXBD	5-22-2009	$19.61	$67.73	246.6%	34.3%
INFOSYS TECHNOLOGY	INFY	1-14-2009	$26.01	$49.68	91.0%	15.2%

JOY GLOBAL INC.	JOY	4-19-2009	$22.55	$49.51	121.1%	20.3%
SHENGDATECH INC.	SDTHQ.PK	7-14-2009	$4.95	$0.00	-100%	TOTAL LOSS
SUPERIOR ENERGY SER.	SPN	10-07-2008	$20.04	$25.29	26.2%	4.9%
USG CORP.	USG	2-04-2009	$11.23	$25.77	129.6%	20.2%
DECKERS OUTDOOR CP	DECK	1-22-2013	$37.87	$58.34	54.1%	121.8%

The portfolio's performance is based on the stock market's closing prices as of Aug. 8, 2013.The gain or loss for each stock does not include dividends that were received for this account.

The worst performer in the portfolio is Shengdatech Inc., a Chinese stock that was listed on the NASDAQ exchange at the time of my purchase. The investment in Shengdatech was a total loss. It seems that even some of the best investors that purchased Chinese stocks have sustained losses from them and some have been heavy losses. I now recommend that you stay away from most foreign stocks, and the fact that many of those businesses report financial results that cannot be trusted is reason enough. It has recently come to light that many Chinese and Indian companies are deceitful when it comes to their accounting standards resulting in Americans investors being wary about investing in them. Shengdatech easily met the requirements of the stress test explained earlier, which proves that even the system of worry-free investing is not foolproof, and neither is any other investment program or system

ENGlobal Corp. is the second-worst performer in the portfolio and like Shengdatech; it has lost most of its value. ENGlobal provides engineering and other professional services principally to the energy sector in the United States and internationally. I'm convinced that it has taken a beating because it deals heavily with new construction and modifications to existing construction or equipment. I suspect that we won't see a turnaround in the stock's performance until the economy is back in full swing and humming along. Of course, there's a chance that the stock may never recover.

Ceradyne Technology is no longer in the portfolio because the company was acquired by 3M in November 2012 for $847 million or $35 per share. My total return from the investment was 48% and my annual rate of return was 10%. I bought shares of Deckers Outdoor Corp. as a replacement to the Ceradyne Technology shares that were sold. I believe that Deckers Outdoor Corp. will turn out to be an outstanding investment.

Coventry Health Care Inc. is no longer in the portfolio because it was acquired by Aetna Inc. in May 2013 as part of a $7.3 billion deal. My shares were sold on May 6 for $49.99 and my total return from the Coventry Health Care investment was 157.2% and my annual rate of return was 25.9%.

The cash position currently stands at 11.5% in my portfolio. When comparing the performance of the portfolio since its inception to that of the S&P 500, my stock portfolio has an annual rate of return of 22.9% and a total return of 137.9% as of August 8, 2013 and the return figures do not include the dividends that were received. With this being my first account that I took seriously when it came to investing, I did not think to keep track of dividend income. I actually took most if not all of the dividends that were received out of the account. The S&P 500 had an annual rate of return of 5.7% and a total return of 30.9% during the same period without dividends being included. None of the return figures have been adjusted for inflation and calculations are based on the inception date of Sept. 15, 2008. When I consider the fact that all purchases for my Personal Worry-Free Stock Portfolio were completed by early 2010 with the exception of Deckers Outdoor Corp., the newest stock added to the portfolio, and the portfolio has achieved such impressive returns, I must say, "Not bad!"

"If you buy stocks at a big discount to value, it doesn't matter what the market does." —Donald Yacktman

MY TRADITIONAL IRA
(MAY 2012 TO AUG. 2013)

After the creation of my Personal Worry-Free Stock Portfolio some time ago, I discovered many excellent stocks that qualified as worry-free stocks for generating great wealth. In May 2012, I lost my job of 22 years. Because of the job loss, I had the opportunity to rollover my 401(k) balance into a Traditional IRA. The truth is, I was glad to have the chance to put my money to work in better investments than those offered by the company. As a matter of fact, my 401(k) would have performed much better if it were not for the actions of our managers who decided on two occasions to change investment management firms to save money. The changes resulted in heavy losses for me and the other employees that had 401(k) plans with our company.

I would have preferred to put the funds into a Roth IRA, but to do so would have required me to pay taxes on the money that would be removed from my 401(k). The payment of all taxes due is required by federal law because the Roth IRA is an after-tax account whereas taxes are commonly deferred on most 401(k) contributions, and such was my case. It's my desire to hold off on paying taxes on my retirement funds for as long as I can while my money compounds tax-free. The portfolio was started on May 22, 2012, and originally contained 16 stocks. Since that time, the number of stocks held in the portfolio has varied with about 20 stocks being the upper limit. Although the account is an IRA, it's still a worry-free stock portfolio that I created according to the principles and strategies contained in this book. When looking at the gains or losses, the numbers may not seem to make sense when comparing the average cost per share to the latest price because the gain or loss figures provided also include dividends that were received and reinvested.

STOCK NAME	STOCK SYMBOL	INITIAL PURCHASE	AVG. COST PER SHARE	LATEST PRICE	GAIN/ LOSS
ALMOST FAMILY INC.	AFAM	5-22-2012	$20.85	$19.52	0.3%
CLIFF NATURAL RESOURCES	CLF	3-18-2013	$19.53	$22.01	13.1%
DECKER OUTDOOR CP	DECK	5-22-2012	$54.15	$58.34	7.0%
EBIX INC.	EBIX	5-22-2012	$19.03	$11.17	-30.7%
EZCORP INC.	EZPW	5-22-2012	$22.27	$17.86	-17.2%
GREEN MOUNT. COFFEE	GMCR	6-18-2012	$20.16	$76.48	243.3%
JINPAN INTL. LTD.	JST	7-03-2012	$7.95	$6.05	-23.0%
JOY GLOBAL INC.	JOY	4-01-2013	$56.43	$49.51	-12.0%
NATIONAL STEEL COMPANY	SID	5-22-2012	$5.28	$3.07	-38.5%
OUTERWALL INC.	OUTR	5-14-2013	$56.96	$60.51	6.2%
QUESTCOR PHARMACEUT.	QCOR	5-13-2013	$39.43	$66.19	67.9%
RPC INC.	RES	5-23-2012	$11.18	$14.75	30.3%
TITAN MACHINERY	TITN	9-12-2012	$21.17	$17.80	-6.4%

The portfolio's performance is based on the stock market's close as of Aug. 8, 2013. The cost basis of the original investments in this newer portfolio is $58,841.99 and the current balance in the portfolio is $81,378.99. This gives the portfolio a total return or gain of $22,537.00, or 38.3%, in about one year and three months, and an annual return rate of 30.7% for this portfolio with dividends reinvested. The S&P 500 had a total return of 32.0% and an annual rate of return of 25.7% with dividends reinvested over the same period of time.

The best performer in the portfolio during the period was Green Mountain Coffee Roasters. Its total return was an amazing 243.3%. Of course, that's nothing compared to what the stock has returned to those that have owned it for several years. According to research, many long-term owners of the stock have made returns of several thousand percent.

Cliffs Natural Resources and National Steel Co. are investments in the portfolio that are commodity stocks and commodity stocks can be very volatile, but I do like these two picks. I originally purchased Cliffs Natural Resources as a coattail investment.

I found Universal Insurance Holdings to be an impressive stock when I begin to look at its financial situation. It was trading in the $3 range, yet it had more than $8 per share in cash and was also paying out hefty dividends to its shareholders.

Stocks that were sold out of the portfolio are Rue21 Inc. with a 37.6% gain, Aecom Technology Corp. with a 73.1% gain, Guess Inc. with a 10.3% gain, Noble Corp. with a 31.8% gain, ManTech International Corp. with a 10.3% gain, UFP Technologies Inc. with a 10.4% gain, Capella Education Co. with a 79.2% gain, Ultra Petroleum Corp. with a 5.1% gain, Jinpan International Ltd. with a 2.0% loss, and Cliffs Natural Resources with a gain of 3.0%. I must admit that there has been a lot more buying and selling activity than I like or had planned.

Note: I used the CAGR Calculator located at *The Online Investor* website (theonlineinvestor.com) to calculate all S&P 500 return figures. I found other online calculators, but they would not allow the input of specific dates, and they also produced S&P 500 return figures that were much lower than the calculator available through *The Online Investor.*

"All you need in a lifetime of successful investing is a few big winners, and the pluses from those will overwhelm the minuses from stocks that don't work out." — Peter Lynch

MY PERSONAL WORRY-FREE STOCK
PORTFOLIO (CURRENT HOLDINGS)

STOCK NAME	STOCK SYMBOL	INITIAL PURCHASE	AVG. COST PER SHARE	LATEST PRICE	GAIN/ LOSS	ANNUAL RETURN
ANIKA THERAPEUTICS	ANIK	3-13-2015	$39.82	$55.86	40.3%	14.4%
CHICAGO BRIDGE & IRON CO.	CBI	3-13-2015	$45.56	$15.05	-67.0%	-35.6%
COACH INC.	COH	1-06-2009	$20.37	$41.40	103.3%	8.5%
COGNIZANT TECHNOLOGY	CTSH	9-15-2008	$10.93	$71.82	557.1%	23.2%
CORPORATE EXECUTIVE	EXBD	5-22-2009	$19.61	$78.75	301.6%	SOLD 3/15/17 19.4%
DECKERS OUTDOOR CORP.	DECK	1-22-2013	$37.85	$63.80	68.6%	11.9%
DXP ENTERPRISES	DXPE	6-02-2009	$13.99	$29.88	113.5%	9.6%
ENGLOBAL CORP.	ENG	7-15-2009	$4.63	$1.39	-70.0%	-13.7%
GILEAD SCIENCES INC.	GILD	8-10-2016	$78.97	$82.36	4.3%	3.9%
INFOSYS TECHNOLOGY	INFY	1-14-2009	$6.50	$14.65	125.3%	9.8%
SUPERIOR ENERGY SER.	SPN	10-07-2008	$20.03	$10.02	-50.0%	-7.4%

THE COOPER COMPANIES, INC.	COO	3-16-2017	$194.22	$245.21	26.3%	58.0%
UNITEDHEALTH GROUP, INC.	UNH	3-16-2017	$170.46	$198.18	16.3%	34.4%
USG CORP.	USG	2-04-2009	$11.22	$30.38	170.8%	12.2%
VMWARE INC.	VMW	3-16-2017	$91.03	$110.25	21.1%	45.6%

The portfolio's performance is based on the stock market's closing prices as of Sept. 15, 2017. The gains or losses for each stock do not include dividends that were received for this account.

The best performer in the portfolio is Cognizant Technology Solutions with a total return of 557.1% and an annual rate of return of 23.2% since its purchase in September 2008.

Cognizant Technology Solutions has also been the best performer in the portfolio since August 2013.

ENGlobal Corp. has been the worst performer in the portfolio since August 2013. It currently has a total loss of 70.0% since its purchase in July 2009.

I sold Joy Global Inc. from the portfolio in July 2016 after learning it had agreed to be acquired by Komatsu Ltd. ADR for $3.7 billion or $28.30 per share. The deal was expected to be completed by mid-2017. My average cost per share for Joy Global was $22.55 and my selling price was $27.95 per share. My total return from this sale was a gain of 23.9% and my annual rate of return from this sale was 3.0%. Some funds obtained from this sell were used to purchase biotechnology company Gilead Sciences Inc.

I sold Corporate Executive Board Co. on March 15, 2017, after learning of an agreed upon acquisition by Gartner Group for $2.6 billion. I paid an average price of $19.61 per share for Corporate Executive Board Co. and sold my share at $78.75 per share for a total return of 301.6% and an annual rate of return of 19.4% and the funds from the sell will be used to add new positions to the portfolio.

I must admit that the performance of this portfolio should be much, much better than it currently stands. Since its inception in 2008, my Personal Worry-Free Stock Portfolio has a total return of 125.6%, as of Sept. 15, 2017. The cash position currently stands at 4.8% and the return figures do not include dividends that were received. The total amount of all contributions made to the account were $48,083.61 and the ending balance is $108,477.91. The S&P 500 has a total return of 82.2% without including dividends that were received during the same period. None of the return figures have been adjusted for inflation. Remember, I have been mostly passive in the management of this portfolio since its inception. I'm now fully and completely convinced that the individual investor should be active in the management of his or her portfolio to achieve the maximum returns possible. By being passive with this account, I gave back some amazing gains I had obtained, and the loss of those gains had a big impact on the long-term performance of this portfolio. Although the portfolio had a total return of 125.6%, the performance would have easily been much better if the account had been actively managed. Let me explain. As of Dec. 31, 2013, the portfolio had a total return of 206.6% and an annual compound rate of return of 27.5%, which proves that the strategies taught in this book work unless you passively invest. You must be active in the management of your portfolio and with the stocks contained in it. Now, I'm going to show you how passive investing can really hurt you using just one real example from this portfolio.

In June 2009, I purchased DXP Enterprises Inc. at an average cost of $14 per share. During my holding period, it traded as high as $116.88 per share. This means that had I sold at its high point, I would have obtained a gain of more than 1,000%. Well, DXP Enterprises is still in this portfolio, and currently trades at $29.88 per share. My total return from this investment now stands at 113.5% instead of more than 1,000%. As an investor, you will never sell at the top except with a little luck, but you should do everything in your power to hold onto as much of your gains as possible by selling stocks when you find them to be extremely overvalued. Just think, DXP Enterprises may never again approach the $116 per share price range and if it does, it may take many years for it to do so.

The great Peter Lynch stated, "All you need for a lifetime of successful investing is a few big winners, and the pluses from those will overwhelm the minuses from the stocks that don't work out." DXP Enterprises is the perfect example of what Lynch meant. Just imagine a few big winners of more than 1,000%, yet, by my continuing to hold DXP Enterprises, the portfolio's performance greatly suffered. If you are like me, then you don't want to continue holding a winning stock until it turns into a losing stock. Sell the overvalued stocks and take your profits. That's the way legendary investor Jim Slater did it. Once more, the individual investor should be active in the management of his or her portfolio to achieve the best returns possible and should consider using index funds and exchange traded funds if they desire to be passive investors.

"It's not whether you're right or you're wrong that's important, but how much money you make when you're right and how much you lose when you're wrong."
—*George Soros*

MY TRADITIONAL IRA (CURRENT HOLDINGS)

STOCK NAME	STOCK SYMBOL	INITIAL PURCHASE	AVG. COST PER SHARE	LATEST PRICE	GAIN/ LOSS
ATWOOD OCEANICS INC.	ATW	5-30-2014	$24.83	$8.02	-65.9%
BED BATH & BEYOND	BBBY	5-12-2017	$34.55	$28.67	-16.7%
BIOGEN INC.	BIIB	5-09-2017	$266.16	$321.26	20.7%
BOFI HOLDINGS	BOFI	9-05-2017	$26.00	$26.29	24.8%
CHICAGO BRIDGE & IRON INC.	CBI	10-07-2014	$39.93	$15.05	-55.7%
COGNIZANT TECH. SOLUTIONS CORP.	CTSH	4-21-2017	$60.55	$71.82	19.0%
DOLLAR GENERAL CORP.	DG	5-02-2017	$71.86	$77.60	8.2%
EXPRESS SCRIPTS HOLDING CO.	ESRX	4-19-2017	$66.16	$62.65	-5.3%
F5 NETWORKS INC.	FFIV	5-16-2017	$129.07	$116.62	-9.6%
FONAR CORP.	FONR	5-01-2017	$20.88	$29.05	39.2%
GEOSPACE TECHNOLOGY CORP.	GEOS	7-28-2014	$23.64	$16.82	-28.8%
ICAHN ENTERPRISES LP	IEP	4-17-2017	$50.54	$54.40	8.2%
LKQ CORP.	LKQ	6-06-2017	$32.31	$35.35	9.4%

T. ROWE PRICE HEALTH FUND	PRHSX	7-05-2017	$70.60	$73.81	4.6%
TITAN MACHINERY	TITN	9-12-2012	$21.17	$14.03	-21.3
TRACTOR SUPPLY COMPANY	TSCO	4-26-2017	$61.39	$63.16	3.6%
TRANSGLOBE ENERGY CORP.	TGA	11-06-2013	$2.66	$1.07	-57.5%
UNDER ARMOUR INC.	UA	4-24-2017	$18.15	$16.46	-9.3%
UNITED THERAPEUTICS CORP.	UTHR	9-11-2017	$121.25	$120.79	16.3 %
VALEANT PHARMACEUTICALS	VRX	10-28-2015	$45.46	$13.92	-69.4%
VANGUARD STAPLES ETF	VDC	7-17-2017	$140.48	$142.11	1.2%

This portfolio's performance is based on the stock market's closing prices as of Sept. 15, 2017. The total amount of all contributions made to the account was $58,841.99, and the ending balance is $135,767.66. This gives the portfolio a total return or gain of $76,925.67, or 130.7%, in about five years and four months. The annual rate of return stands at 17.0% for this portfolio during that period. The portfolio's returns also include dividends that were reinvested. The S&P 500 had a total return of 111.0%, and an annual compound return rate of 15.1% with dividends reinvested during the same period.

"The stock market is inherently misleading. Doing what everybody else is doing can often be wrong." —Charles Brandes

RECENT TRADITIONAL IRA TRANSACTIONS

In January 2014, I decided to add this section because I felt it would be very beneficial for you to see how I have made some of my decisions when it comes to buying and selling stocks. All buy and sell transactions are from my Traditional IRA since I'm mostly a passive investor when it comes to my Personal Worry-Free Stock Portfolio. As an investor, I don't expect it's possible to buy or sell a stock at the perfect time but it's easily possible to buy or sell at the wrong time. I have come to realize that there will be times when I'm going to sell too early or too late and if you invest long enough so will you. If I sell a stock after I have made a good profit, I don't care if it continues to climb in value after I have sold it. Remember this: when it comes to profiting from stocks, no one knows it all. So, learn to be content with the profits that you make and don't allow greed to cause you to do something unwise. When you make a mistake, learn from it. What's foolish is to keep making the same mistakes again and again. Finally, it's just as important for an investor to understand why he or she sold a specific stock as well as why he or she bought it.

Universal Insurance Holdings Inc. (UVE) Sold Out: January 2014

I bought Universal Insurance Holdings in May 2012 for an average cost of $3.62 per share. I found Universal Insurance Holdings through the FINVIZ stock screener. Universal Insurance Holdings had very good fundamentals, but what originally attracted me to the stock was the fact that it was trading in the $3 price range, yet it had more than $8 per share in cash. I sold it when its cash per share dropped down to the $3 range, but the stock was up significantly above its cash per share position. At the average purchase price of $3.62 per share and the selling price of $13.64 per share, my total return from the investment was 276.8% with an annual rate of return of

121%. I also received a huge amount of dividend income from this stock, which almost made me hate to sell it.

Questcor Pharmaceuticals Inc. (QCOR) Increased Position: January 2014

I already held Questcor Pharmaceuticals in my portfolio but decided to add to my position. I purchased my original shares at an average cost of $42.61 per share, and added to the position at an average cost of $54.84 per share. I was glad to add to my position of this stock because I believe Questcor is capable of growing its earnings per share by a minimum of 28% annually over the long term. Its five-year average returns on equity and capital stood at 63%, and I estimated its fair value to be from $138.60 to $141.17 per share.

Joy Global Inc. (JOY) Increased Position: January 2014

I already held Joy Global in my portfolio but decided to add to my position. I paid from $56.39 to $59.41 for the original shares. This purchase cost me $55.62 per share. Although I don't see tremendous overall growth with Joy Global, I think that it's a good, solid pick. It has managed to grow its book value by more than 25% annually over the last seven to 10 years. It has an impressive five-year average return on equity of 43% and a five-year average return on capital of 22%. I estimate that it's capable of growing its earnings about 11% annually over the long term. I also estimate that it has a fair value of between $72.27 per share and $85.50 per share.

Sturm, Ruger & Co. (RGR) New Position: March 2014

Sturm, Ruger & Co. is a new stock that was added to my portfolio. I bought it because I think that it's an extremely undervalued stock. I think that it's easily capable of long-term earnings per share growth rate of more than 30%. It managed to grow its EPS at an annual rate of more than 47% for the last five years. Its managers are extremely effective in their use of the shareholders' retained earnings. The long-term return on retained earnings is 52% and the five-year average returns on capital and equity stands at about 47%. I estimated Sturm, Ruger & Co. to have a minimum fair value of

$107.04 and a maximum fair value of $139.72. My average cost per share for Sturm, Ruger & Co. stands at $64.51.

Geospace Technologies Corp. (GEOS) New Position: May 2014

Geospace Technologies Corp. is a new stock that was added to my portfolio. When I'm able to find solid performing technology businesses that are not hard to understand, I will buy them when the price is right. Geospace Technologies has no long-term debt. Its five-year average return on equity and return on capital stands at 15%, and its five-year earnings per share growth rate stands at 36%. I estimated Geospace Technologies to have a fair value of $74.31 to $89.68 per share. My average cost per share for Geospace Technologies is $50.96. Even if the low side estimate is correct, I believe that the stock has upside potential of about 46% within the next few years at the price that I paid for my shares.

Atwood Oceanics Inc. (ATW) New Position: May 2014

Atwood Oceanics Inc. is a new stock that was added to my portfolio. I have been watching this stock for some time now. The company has long-term debt that is within the limits that I like. Although Atwood Oceanics only managed to grow its earnings per share by 11% annually over the last five years, analysts are estimating that the long-term EPS growth rate will be 20% annually. Atwood Oceanics has grown its book value by more than 24% annually for the last 7-10 years. If analysts are correct, I estimate that Atwood Oceanics has a fair value of $115.52 to $121.60 per share. I paid an average price of $49.33 per share. If my estimate is correct, the stock has tremendous upside potential plus a large margin of safety at the price that I paid.

Keurig Green Mountain Inc. (GMCR) Reduced Position: July 2014

There's a saying when it comes to investing, "Sell your losers and let your profits ride." What this really means is that an investor should hold on to his or her winning stocks and only rid his or her portfolio of losers. Most investors appear to hold on to the losing stocks in their portfolio and get rid of the winners with the hope that the losing stocks will someday recover. What they eventually end up with is a portfolio filled with losing stocks. I seriously wanted to make sure I wasn't making the same mistake by selling my shares of Keurig Green Mountain Inc. Keurig Green Mountain was formerly known as Green Mountain Coffee Roasters Inc., and that's what you will find it listed as in my Traditional IRA (MAY 2012 TO AUG. 2013) that was presented earlier. I purchased most of my shares of Keurig Green Mountain in June 2012, but also purchased a smaller number in July and August of the same year. I decided to take some profits by selling only half of my shares because even now I keep hearing a lot of good things about the business. Analysts estimated Keurig Green Mountain should earn $3.78 for 2014, and that it should grow its long-term EPS by 17% annually. I personally think Keurig Green Mountain will do much better than the analysts are estimating. It managed to grow it EPS at an annual rate of almost 65% over the most recent five-year period. If analysts are correct, it's time to dump all of my shares, but I don't think they are. So, that's why I decided to sell only half of my shares. I'm going to continue to let the profits ride on the remaining shares. My average cost per share was $20.16 and my selling price was $122.62 per share. My total return from the sell was 508.3% and my annual rate of return was 137.9%. With the shares that I have left, I will reassess the business every few months and will re-estimate the stock's fair value. When I think the stock is too expensive, I will sell. At the moment, I think that Keurig Green Mountain is fairly priced, but I also think it has more room to run.

Questcor Pharmaceuticals Inc. (QCOR) Sold Out: July 2014

The situation with Questcor Pharmaceuticals Inc. is the perfect example of why "buy and hold" does not mean "buy and forget." Keeping a check on the status of all the businesses that you are invested in is an essential component to your success as an investor. While doing some research on the statuses of my stocks to see if anything important had occurred, I discovered that Questcor Pharmaceuticals had agreed to a merger with Mallinckrodt Pharmaceuticals, a specialty drug manufacturer. The merger was to be completed in August 2014. Here's my problem with the whole situation: I bought Questcor Pharmaceuticals on the basis of the information that I knew about it, and estimated its fair value accordingly. When it comes to Mallinckrodt, I haven't the slightest idea of how to place an intrinsic value on it with the limited information I've been able to find. It's also a foreign company that's headquartered in Ireland, and I have not done well with most of the foreign investments I have owned in the past. When I look at the bigger picture, I don't know whether the new company that will be created through the merger will be a success or failure. Uncertainty about the new company's future made my decision to sell Questcor Pharmaceuticals an easy one. My average cost per share for Questcor Pharmaceuticals was $43.89 and my selling price was $96.26 per share. My total return from the sell was 119.3% and my annual rate of return was 96.0%. The figures do not include the $152.95 in dividends that I received from my Questcor Pharmaceuticals shares. If we were to add the dividends into the above figures, my real returns would be even more impressive — and that's a stock that I owned for only about fourteen months.

Atwood Oceanics Inc. (ATW) Increased Position: July 2014

I purchased these shares of Atwood Oceanics at an average cost of $49.27 per share.

Sturm, Ruger & Co. (RGR) Increased Position: July 2014

I paid an average price of $58.20 per share for this purchase.

Geospace Technologies Corp. (GEOS) Increased Position: July 2014

I paid an average price of $43.31 per share for this purchase.

Outerwall Inc. (OUTR) Increased Position: July 2014

I paid an average price of $53.28 per share for this purchase.

Deckers Outdoor Corp. (DECK) Sold Out: August 2014

I began my purchase of shares of Deckers Outdoor Corp. in May 2012, and increased my share position up through July 2013. Analysts estimated Deckers Outdoor Corp.'s long-term EPS growth rate would be 13.5%, and that the company would earn $4.68 per share in 2014. I estimated that Deckers Outdoor Corp. would perform slightly differently. My estimates were that Deckers Outdoor Corp. would grow its EPS at a long-term rate of 15.9% and that its EPS for 2014 would be $4.61 per share. Based on my analysis, I estimated Deckers Outdoor Corp.'s fair value to be from $73.30 to $78.14 per share. With Deckers Outdoor Corp. trading at $88.31 per share, I decided to sell since the shares were overvalued. My average cost per share for Deckers Outdoor Corp. was $53.25 and my selling price was $88.31 per share. My total return from the sell was a gain of 65.8% and my annual rate of return for these shares was 43.1%. Again, my main reason for selling these shares was because they were overvalued based on the metrics that I use. The PEG Ratio for these shares also stood at 1.22 at the time of my sell.

National Steel Co. (SID) Sold Out: August 2014

I sold National Steel Co. because I'm in the process of building up my cash reserve. My average cost per share was $5.00 and my selling price per share was $5.11 for National Steel Co. So, there was very little gain in the way of price appreciation, but I did receive $421.80 in dividends for my shares, which resulted in a total return of 7.9% and an annual return rate of 8.9% on my investment.

EZCORP Inc. (EZPW) Increased Position: August 2014

I purchased these newer shares of EZCORP at an average cost of $9.70 per share. My original shares cost $22.27 per share, which means that my original shares have lost more than 56% of their value. A shakeup in management resulted in EZCORP's most recent tumble in price.

Coach Inc. (COH) New Position: August 2014

Coach Inc. is a new stock that has been added to this portfolio, although I have held shares in my Personal Worry-Free Stock Portfolio for a long time. I completed a new analysis of Coach Inc. in April 2013 and have not bothered to complete another one. At the time, Coach was trading for $55.55 per share, and had managed to grow its EPS at an annual rate of 16% for its most recent five-year period at that time. Analysts also estimated that Coach would grow its long-term earnings per share at a rate of 13% annually. Coach's returns on capital and equity over the long term stood at 49%, and Coach had also managed to grow its book value over the long term by more than 21% and its return on retained earnings also stood at 43% at the time. In 2013, I estimated Coach Inc. had a fair value from $51.87 to $61.85 per share. My purchase price of Coach is $36.92 per share. So, if my estimates pan out, these shares are a real bargain.

Lululemon Athletica Inc. (LULU) New Position: August 2014

Lululemon Athletica Inc. reminded me so much of Keurig Green Mountain when an analysis was performed on the company. The stock is way off of its 52-week high of more than $80 per share and I purchased shares for my account at an average price of $40.70 per share. Lululemon Athletica has no debt and its five-year EPS growth rate stands at about 46%. Its return on retained earnings is about 28% and its returns on capital and equity are 34%. Lululemon Athletica has also grown its book value by an annual rate of more than 41% over the long term. I estimate Lululemon Athletica to have a fair value from $56.64 to $74.12 per share.

RPC Inc. (RES) Sold Out: September 2014

I purchased my initial shares of RPC Inc. in May 2012 and continued to build my position in the stock up through January 2014. I based my purchase on an analysis I performed in 2012 for the 2013 year. I estimated that RPC Inc. would have earnings of $1.43 per share for 2013, and that it was capable of growing its EPS by a long-term rate of 18%. I also estimated that RPC Inc. had a fair value of $25.53 to $25.88 at that time. I don't remember what the analysts' exact estimates were, but I do know we were all way off on our estimates. In 2013, RPC Inc. earned only $0.77 per share or about half of what I and the analysts figured that it would; and yet, the stock has still managed to reach a price that I'm comfortable selling my shares at. My average cost per share for RPC Inc. was $12.44 and my selling price was $22.75 per share. My total return from the sell was a gain of 82.9% and my annual rate of return for these shares was 69.3%. I also received a total of $323.20 in dividends during my ownership of RPC Inc. My main reason for the sale of my shares was because I believed that the shares were trading near to their fair value.

Note: In March 2015, RPC Inc.'s shares traded as low as $11.49 per share, which means that had I not sold, I would have lost all of my gains and some of my invested money.

Coach Inc. (COH) Increased Position: September 2014

I purchased these shares of Coach Inc. at an average price of $37.38 per share.

Lululemon Athletica Inc. (LULU) Increased Position: September 2014

I purchased these shares at an average price of $38.96.

Atwood Oceanics Inc. (ATW) Increased Position: September 2014

I purchased these shares of Atwood Oceanics Inc. at an average price of $46.37 per share.

Sturm, Ruger & Co. (RGR) Increased Position: September 2014

I paid an average price of $51.67 per share for this purchase.

Geospace Technologies Corp. (GEOS) Increased Position: September 2014

I paid an average price of $39.52 per share for this purchase.

Outerwall Inc. (OUTR) Increased Position: September 2014

I paid an average price of $60.55 per share for this purchase.

Chicago Bridge & Iron Co. (CBI) New Position: October 2014

Chicago Bridge & Iron Co. is a company that I have kept an eye on for several years, but it had been too expensive for my purchase until now. It has grown its EPS by more than 25% annually for the last five years. Its five-year average return on equity stands at 23% and its five-year average return on capital stands at 20%. During the last seven to 10 years, Chicago Bridge & Iron's book value has grown at an annual rate of more than 18%. Analysts estimate Chicago Bridge & Iron will grow its EPS at an annual rate of 15% over the long term. I estimate that it will do a little better and will grow its EPS at an annual rate of 19% over the long term. Of course, I could be wrong. Based on my estimate, Chicago Bridge & Iron has a fair value of $87.77 to $89.67, and I purchased shares for my portfolio at an average price of $54.60 per share. My margin of safety stands at almost 38% for this purchase. The Motley Fool Caps community also has assigned Chicago Bridge & Iron a rating of 4 stars out of 5.

Keurig Green Mountain Inc. (GMCR) Sold Out: October 2014

I decided to go ahead and sell the remaining half of my Keurig Green Mountain shares because I estimated that the shares had become overvalued. Analysts estimated Keurig Green Mountain would earn $3.76 for 2014, and that it would grow its EPS at a long-term rate of 17% annually. I believe it's capable of performing much better than the analysts are estimating and I can see it achieving a long-term EPS growth rate of 20% annually. Using my own EPS growth rate estimate of 20% would give Keurig Green Mountain an EPS estimate of $3.79 for 2014 and $4.55 for 2015. Analysts estimated EPS of about $4.00 for 2015, which is much lower than my estimate. Even if my higher estimates are correct, the shares have become overvalued. For example, using the modified PEG ratio would give a fair value of $91 for 2015. Do you remember the following formula for the modified PEG ratio?

$4.55 (2015 EPS Estimate) X 20 (5 Year Earnings Growth Rate Estimate) = $91.00 (Fair Value)

My average cost per share for the remaining shares was $19.62 and my selling price was $140.10 per share. My total return from the sell was 614.1% and my annual rate of return was 139.6%. The only regret that I have about Keurig Green Mountain is not buying more shares when the stock was still cheap. Overall, I'm very happy with the returns that I have earned from Keurig Green Mountain.

Note: On July 8, 2015, Keurig Green Mountain's shares traded as low as $70.51 per share. Do you think that I made the right decision to sell?

eBay Inc. (EBAY) New Position: October 2014

I did not purchase eBay Inc. a few years ago when it was trading for less than $27 per share. Since then, eBay is currently up more than 100% in price. Although I failed to purchase eBay back then, I decided I wasn't going to make the same mistake twice and added eBay Inc. to my portfolio as a coattail investment. I recently learned that eBay is planning to spin off PayPal, its payment processing business. While further researching eBay at GuruFocus.com, I found that many of the pros had been loading up on its shares. Seth Klarman, Wallace Weitz, Carl Icahn, Joel Greenblatt, George Soros and Ken Fisher are just a few of the investors who recently bought shares of eBay's stock; and when you see investors of their caliber buying a particular stock, they know something about the business that we don't. According to GuruFocus.com, eBay's stock traded in the price range of $48.25 to $56.04 with its average price being $51.79 during the purchases by those great investors mentioned. I purchased my shares of eBay at an average cost of $51.41 per share.

Chicago Bridge & Iron Co. (CBI) Increased Position: December 2014

After my initial purchase of shares of Chicago Bridge & Iron Co., the stock took a serious tumble in price and fell as low as $37.37 per share. As investor, that's something that we have no control over, but by splitting up our purchases over three to four buy periods and only buying more of a specific stock when its price is lower than our previous purchase price, we lower our average cost per share for our purchases and increase our margin of safety. I like to reassess my reason for purchasing a specific stock after it has fallen in price like Chicago Bridge & Iron did.

If the story has not changed, I continue holding the stock. I purchased the initial shares of Chicago Bridge & Iron for my portfolio at an average price of $54.60 per share and these newer shares were purchased at an average price of $42.35 per share.

Almost Family Inc. (AFAM) Sold Out: January 2015

I purchased my initial shares of Almost Family Inc. in May 2012 and continued to build my position in the stock up through May 2014. I did sell some of the shares on a few occasions in 2012 and 2013 to raise my cash position in my account for some other purchases. My main reason for selling out my remaining position in Almost Family Inc. was because I wanted to put the available funds into what I believe to be a much better investment. My average cost per share for Almost Family Inc. was $21.20 and my selling price was $28.26 per share. My total return from the sell was a gain of 33.3% and my annual rate of return for these shares was 23.5%. I also received a total of $328.20 in dividends during my ownership of Almost Family Inc. By the way, I still think that Almost Family Inc. is a very good, solid pick to hold for the long term — unless, of course, you can find a much better stock to invest your money in.

Note: Almost Family Inc. reached the trading price of $49.60 on April 14, 2015. I could kick myself for selling too soon, but the truth is that no one knows when a stock will take off as Almost Family Inc. has done. So, don't be too hard on yourself when a stock climbs in price after you sell it. Had I held on to Almost Family until the $49.60, I would have obtained a total return from the investment of about 134%.

Ebix Inc. (EBIX) Sold Out: January 2015

I begin my purchase of shares of Ebix Inc. in May 2012 and completed the purchase of most of my shares in the same year. I had estimated that Ebix would grow its EPS at a long-term annual rate of 20%. I had also estimated that Ebix was worth about $43.00 to $44.00 per share in 2012. It may reach my estimate of its fair value, but it will do so without my ownership. I have a few reasons that led to my decision to sell Ebix. First, I concluded that Ebix is not the investor friendly company that I originally thought it was. For example, in 2013, Ebix agreed to be bought out and taken private by Goldman Sachs in an all-cash deal of about $20 per share. The deal was terminated because shareholders filed a class action lawsuit against Ebix's directors and officers, accusing them of intentional misconduct. Next, there have been too many issues surrounding Ebix's accounting practices within the last few years resulting in investigations from both the Department of Justice and the Securities and Exchange Commission. Finally, the stock has not performed as well as I figured that it would do during my holding period. My average cost per share for Ebix Inc. was $19.03 and my selling price was $19.53 per share. As you can see, I didn't make much with this investment. My total return from the sell was 7.2% and my annual rate of return for these shares was 3.3%. I received a total of $97.00 in dividends and that amount was included in both return figures just mentioned.

Anika Therapeutics Inc. (ANIK) New Position: January 2015

Anika Therapeutics is one company that I somehow missed earlier when it was trading at an even better price than what I paid for these shares. In January 2013, this stock could have been bought for about $10 per share, which would have given an investor about a 300% return on his or her investment in a little more than two years. I checked Anika Therapeutics out a few years ago but have no idea why I didn't buy shares at the time. Recently, I have really come to like biotechnology and healthcare stocks. Anika Therapeutics has no long-term debt and has grown its EPS at an annual rate of 35% for the most recent five-year period. Anika Therapeutics has also managed to grow its book value at an annual rate of about 14% over the last 7-10 years. Its five-year average return on equity is 10% and its five-year average return on capital is about 9%.

With this stock, I loosened my 15% minimum concerning its return on equity and its return on capital. Analysts estimate that Anika Therapeutics will grow its EPS at a long-term annual rate of 30%. I wasn't as optimistic with my EPS estimate and assigned a lower long-term rate of 26.3% for Anika Therapeutics. For 2014, Anika Therapeutics is expected to earn $2.45 per share. Although it's 2015, Anika Therapeutics has not reported its yearly financial results for 2014 yet. My taking into consideration its 2014 EPS estimate, I estimate that Anika Therapeutics has a fair value of $65.12 to $77.59 per share. I bought these initial shares at an average price of $39.52 per share. The Motley Fool's Caps community has assigned the stock 3 stars out of a possible 5 stars.

DXP Enterprises Inc. (DXPE) New Position: January 2015

DXP Enterprises Inc. is a stock that I have held in my Personal Worry-Free Stock Portfolio since June 2009, and I purchased those shares at an average cost of $14.00 per share. By December 2013, DXP Enterprises shares were trading as high as $112 per share. I knew the shares were overvalued at that point, but decided not to sell because I wanted to see how well the portfolio would do over the long term with minimal selling of shares and was determined to sell only as a last resort. I paid $41.61 per share for the shares I purchased for this account. DXP Enterprises has grown its EPS at an annual rate of about 24% for the last five years, and I estimate it will grow its EPS at an annual rate of 21% over the long term. Although its five-year rates for its return on equity and return on capital are unimpressive, management has been very effective with its use of retained earnings and has produced a long-term return on retained earnings of more than 30%. Management has also grown DXP Enterprises' book value at an annual rate of more than 33% over the long term. I estimate DXP Enterprises' fair value to be from $88.53 to $95.34 per share at the time of this purchase.

Anika Therapeutics Inc. (ANIK) Increased Position: February 2015

I purchased these shares at an average price of $39.21 per share.

PRA Group Inc. (PRAA) New Position: January 2015

PRA Group Inc., formerly known as Portfolio Recovery Associates, is a stock that I discovered several years ago. Since then, the shares are up several hundred percent when an adjustment for its 2013 stock split is taken into account. Even with its excellent performance and price appreciation, I think there's more profits to be gained for the long-term holders of this stock. PRA Group's EPS growth rate for the last five years was about 33%, and I estimate it will grow its EPS at an annual rate of 21.3% over the next five years. My estimate is higher than the average estimate provided by the analysts, which estimate that PRA Group will grow its EPS at an annual rate of 15%. PRA Group's management has made effective use of the retained earnings with a long-term return on retained earnings of 19%. PRA Group's five-year average return on equity is 20% and its five-year return on capital is 13%. PRA Group's long-term book value growth rate stands at about 19%. I estimate PRA Group's current fair value to be $90.39 to $97.98 per share. I paid an average price of $53.23 per share for my purchase of PRA Group Inc.

DXP Enterprises Inc. (DXPE) Increased Position: March 2015

I paid an average price of $44.60 per share for this purchase.

PRA Group Inc. (PRAA) Increased Position: March 2015

I paid an average price of $51.99 per share for this purchase.

TransGlobe Energy Co. (TGA) Increased Position: March 2015

I purchased my original shares of TransGlobe Energy Co. in November 2013 at an average price of $9.33 per share. TransGlobe Energy is an independent oil and gas company that's headquartered in Calgary, Canada. Most of TransGlobe Energy's oil and gas exploration takes place in very volatile regions of the Middle East, which presents a greater risk for those investors that hold shares of its stock in comparison to independent oil and gas companies located in North America and Europe. Looking at the numbers, the company appears to be a solid pick, but because of the greater risk it presents, I originally bought only a very small position of this stock. When I look at TransGlobe Energy now, even with the stock down about 68% since my original purchase, I don't think the story has changed much for this company and that's the reason that I'm now purchasing additional shares. In November 2013, I estimated TransGlobe Energy Co.'s fair value to be from $19.05 to $20.96 per share. The stock has taken quite a tumble since my original purchase. Of course, the entire oil and gas industry has taken a serious tumble. I paid an average cost of $3.02 per share for this newest purchase.

Anika Therapeutics Inc. (ANIK) Increased Position: March 2015

I paid an average price of $40.07 per share for this purchase.

Orbital ATK Inc. (OA) New Position: March 2015

Orbital ATK serves the aerospace and defense industries and I thought that it would be a good fit within my portfolio by providing a little more diversification to the portfolio. I realize that Sturm, Ruger & Co. Inc., a company whose shares I already own, serves the aerospace and defense industries as well. The difference is that Orbital ATK deals in complex and sophisticated firearms, rocket motors, missile defense and other high technology defense systems whereas Sturm, Ruger & Co. deals primarily in firearms such as rifles and pistols, which the military refers to as small arms. Orbital ATK has almost no long-term debt and has managed to grow its EPS at an annual rate of almost 14% over the most recent five-year period. Orbital ATK also has grown its book value at an annual rate of 13% over the long term. Its five-year average return on equity stands at 22% and its five-year average return on capital stands at 12%. Presently, Orbital ATK carries a 5-star rating under Motley Fool's Caps rating system. Analysts also estimate that Orbital ATK will grow its EPS at an annual rate of 13.6% over the long term and my estimate is in line with the analysts' estimates. Based on that information, I estimate Orbital ATK to have a fair value of $120.42 to $140.49 per share. With my purchase price of $74.94 per share, I believe Orbital ATK's shares were a real steal.

Outerwall Inc. (OUTR) Reduced Position: April 2015

I sold about 40% of my shares of Outerwall Inc. because it was my largest position in the portfolio, which was not the result of the stock's performance but because of the large amount of money I had invested to build my position in this stock. I decided it was time to reduce my position and use the funds to add to other positions that I hold in the portfolio that I like as much as Outerwall Inc. My average cost per share was $57.95 for these shares and my selling price was $67.57 per share. My total return from the sell was 16.6% and my annual rate of return was 8.3%.

Anika Therapeutics Inc. (ANIK) Increased Position: April 2015

I purchased these shares at an average price of $38.89 per share.

DXP Enterprises Inc. (DXPE) Increased Position: April 2015

I paid an average price of $45.12 per share for this purchase.

PRA Group Inc. (PRAA) Increased Position: April 2015

I purchased these shares of PRA Group at an average cost of $55.39 per share.

TransGlobe Energy Co. (TGA) Increased Position: April 2015

I paid an average price of $4.31 per share for this purchase.

Michael Kors Holdings Ltd. (KORS) New Position: April 2015

Michael Kors Holdings Ltd. is a global provider of luxury accessories, footwear, and apparel. Michael Kors, headquartered in Hong Kong, was founded in 1981 and went public in December 2011. Shares of Michael Kors have fallen more than 33% over the last year. Michael Kors grew its EPS at an annual rate of about 76% during the most recent five-year period. Of course, I don't expect a repeat of that amazing feat and neither do other investors, and that's the main reason the shares have fallen so much in price. Michael Kors' five-year average return on equity stands at an impressive 47% and its five-year average return on capital stands at an impressive 42%. Analysts estimate that Michael Kors will grow its EPS at a long-term annual rate of about 21% and my estimate is slightly higher at 21.3%. The Motley Fool has assigned Michael Kors 4 stars out of a possible 5 and the Motley Fool also owns shares of the stock. Analysts have estimated Michael Kors will earn $4.29 per share for the 2015 year, but I estimate an EPS of $3.72 for 2015. My estimate gives Michael Kors a fair value of $73.10 to $79.24 per share. I realize that the 25% minimum margin of safety isn't there with this purchase, and that there's a good chance that this stock will fall further in price. If it does, hopefully I will get to purchase additionally shares at a much lower price. I purchased these shares for my account at the average price of $63.36 per share.

Michael Kors Holdings Ltd. (KORS) Increased Position: May 2015

I purchased these shares at an average price of $62.41 per share.

Lululemon Athletica Inc. (LULU) Reduced Position: May 2015

I purchased shares for my account at an average price of $40.76 per share. I decided to sell about 20% of my shares of this stock to reduce my position a little and to increase my cash position since my cash position has fallen because of recent purchases. I sold these shares at an average price of $60.56 per share. My total return from the sell was 48.6% and my annual rate of return was 69.5%.

Outerwall Inc. (OUTR) Reduced Position: May 2015

I purchased shares of Outerwall Inc. at an average price of $63.10 per share. I decided to reduce my position of these shares for the same reason that I sold some of Lululemon Athletica shares. I sold about 17% of these shares at an average price of $78.67. My total return from the sell was 24.7% and my annual rate of return for this sell was 12.8%.

Michael Kors Holdings Ltd. (KORS) Increased Position: June 2015

This is my third purchase of shares of Michael Kors Holdings, and I think now is a good time to explain something that may seem odd to you. Any time a stock is sold, there has to be someone on the other end of the trade who bought it; and any time a stock is bought, there must be a seller on the other end. Think about this! When a stock is falling in price, there are more sellers than buyers and the lack of demand drives the stock's price down. On the other hand, when a stock is climbing in price there are more buyers than there are sellers, the additional demand drives the price of a stock up. Most investors think backwards. Here's what I mean: They only want to buy a stock when it is climbing in price, and most investors lose interest in a stock that seems to be falling in price. Remember, to succeed at investing, you got to respond differently than the crowd. You cannot adopt the "herd mentality" and think that you are going to come out ahead of the crowd. I completed my first purchase in April, and in less than two months, the shares have fallen drastically in price with much of the price drop taking place on a single day. On May 27, 2015, Michaels Kors shares opened at $60.59 per share on the market; and at the market's close, the shares traded or closed at $45.93 per share. So, the shares lost more than 24% of their value in a single day. Do you think that something has changed so much at Michael Kors that its shares warrant such a large drop-in price? I seriously doubt it! I paid an average price of $46.87 for this most recent purchase and that really excites me because I simply refuse to follow the crowd since they usually get it wrong!

PRA Group Inc. (PRAA) Increased Position: June 2015

I purchased these shares of PRA Group at an average cost of $58.91 per share.

Anika Therapeutics Inc. (ANIK) Increased Position: June 2015

I purchased these shares at an average price of $33.23 per share.

DXP Enterprises Inc. (DXPE) Increased Position: June 2015

I paid an average price of $42.02 per share for this purchase.

Lululemon Athletica Inc. (LULU) Sold Out: July 2015

I decided to sell the rest of my shares of this stock because the stock had risen more than 63% in price and the margin of safety had decreased drastically with these shares. I had estimated Lululemon Athletica's fair value to be $56.64 to $74.12 per share if the company performed as I estimated for 2014. Well, I was way off on my estimate, but that's OK. There have been some serious issues at the company with some of its products, such as the recent recall of 318,000 hoodies, but new management seems to have now gotten the company headed in the right direction. Even if the stock is worth $74.12 per share, my margin of safety with these shares only stood at about 12% of my selling price. I sold these shares at an average price of $65.15 per share. My total return from the sell was 63.1% and my annual rate of return was 80.1%.

Orbital ATK Inc. (OA) Increased Position: July 2015

For this purchase, I paid an average price of $72.53 per share.

Michael Kors Holdings Ltd. (KORS) Increased Position: July 2015

I paid an average price of $44.16 per share for this purchase.

Chicago Bridge & Iron Co. (CBI) Increased Position: July 2015

I paid an average price of $46.94 per share for this purchase.

Coach Inc. (COH) Increased Position: July 2015

I paid an average price of $33.54 per share for this purchase.

PayPal Holdings Inc. (PYPL) New Position: July 2015

EBay Inc. completed its spinoff of its PayPal division as planned. So, in reality, I did not purchase these shares but they were issued to me as a result of the spinoff. For each share of eBay stock that investors owned, they received one share of PayPal Holdings Inc. At the completion of the spinoff, PayPal's market capitalization was actually much larger than eBay's. That can happen because the company that's created from the spinoff extracts some of the value from the parent company since the parent company is, in reality, shedding some of its assets and liabilities. My cost basis for the PayPal shares is $30.17 per share and my cost basis for the eBay shares is $21.32 per share. I am unable to provide estimates of the fair values of either company at this time, but one thing is for certain: both companies are worth more than my costs per share for them. Eddy Elfenbein, successful investor and editor of *Crossing Wall Street*, has added both PayPal Holdings Inc. and eBay Inc. to his 2015 buy list. He recommends investors should buy eBay below $30 per share and buy PayPal below $42 per share. Mr. Elfenbein's buy list has beaten the S&P 500 seven years out of the last nine between 2006 through 2014. His buy list has also achieved a total return of 151.3% compared to a total return of 99.7% for the S&P 500 over the same period. Check out Elfenbein's website and blog at CrossingWallStreet.com. I'll bet that you will really like his website and his blog.

Keurig Green Mountain Inc. (GMCR) New Position: August 2015

I sold out of my position in Keurig Green Mountain Inc. in October 2014.

Keurig Green Mountain's share have fallen drastically in price since my sell because the company reported disappointing results for the third quarter of 2015, along with some negative revisions of its earnings consensus for 2015. As a result, the shares fell more than 30% in one day. In 2014, using the PEG ratio, I estimated Keurig Green Mountain would have a fair value of $91 for the 2015 fiscal year — and I was way off on my estimate. If it makes you feel better, you should know that the analysts didn't do much better with their estimates. (At least, that makes me feel better!) I decided to keep things a little simpler this time by going to Morningstar to get an idea of Keurig Green Mountain's valuation. According to Morningstar, Keurig Green Mountain has traded at an average P/E ratio of 42.9 over the most recent five-year period. When I learned that its current P/E ratio was 15.6, I knew it was time for me to start buying the stock again. I paid an average price of $53.61 per share this time around.

Outerwall Inc. (OUTR) Sold Out: August 2015

I decided to sell my position in Outerwall Inc. at this time, although I think that it's a very good stock to own if you are a patient investor. Just a few weeks ago, this stock reached a 52-week high and a five-year high of $85.26 per share, and I missed the opportunity to sell my shares at that time. My only reason for selling these shares is because I think that I have some better investment opportunities in some other shares that have fallen in price, such as Keurig Green Mountain. My average cost per share for Outerwall Inc. was $56.45 and my selling price was $62.62 per share. My total return from the sale of my shares was 10.9% and my annual rate of return was 9.9%, which is a very good return considering the short amount of time I held these shares in my account.

Sturm, Ruger & Co. (RGR) Sold Out: August 2015

I decided to sell Sturm Ruger & Co. for much the same reason that I sold Outerwall Inc., which is my belief that there are some better investment choices available now and on the horizon because of the recent market volatility. On Aug. 24, the Dow Jones Industrial Average opened with a

1,000-point drop. It was the biggest intraday move in the Dow's history. My selling was not motivated by fear or in response to the herd; I'm simply convinced that some fantastic stocks are going to get a lot cheaper before the smoke clears, and I want to be ready. I paid an average price of $58.37 per share for these shares and sold them at an average price of $59.29 per share. So, I didn't have much of a gain from selling these shares prematurely. During my ownership, the shares traded as low as $33.60 per share, or at a loss of a little more than 42%, before recovering. My total return from this sell was 1.6% and my annual rate of return was 1.3%. I also received dividends that totaled $223.62 during my ownership of these shares.

Freeport-McMoRan Inc. (FCX) New Position: August 2015

After I considered how beaten down the oil and commodities sectors were this year, I thought it was time for me to add a commodity stock to my portfolio. I really like Freeport-McMoRan Inc., especially at its current trading price of around $10 per share. Freeport-McMoRan is one of the world's largest natural resource companies. It engages in the acquisition of mineral assets as well as oil and natural gas resources. When I look at the various assets of Freeport-McMoRan Inc., I cannot help but to be impressed. I don't feel comfortable providing an estimate of Freeport-McMoRan's fair value because of its history of inconsistent earnings or its inconsistent earnings growth rate to be more specific. This is one of those few stocks that I'm willing to go out on a limb and say that it's intrinsically worth a lot more than its current trading price. I paid an average of $10.23 per share for this initial purchase. I want to also mention that the last time I estimated Freeport-McMoRan's fair value was in October 2011. At that time, EPS was expected to grow at a long-term rate of about 23% annually, and I estimated that Freeport-McMoRan had a fair value of $90.53 to $123.05 per share. In 2011, Freeport-McMoRan earned $4.84 per share. Of course, things have changed since then, and Freeport-McMoRan is expected to earn only $0.42 per share for the 2015 year.

Freeport-McMoRan Inc. (FCX) Increased Position: September 2015

I paid an average price of $9.66 per share for this purchase.

Whole Foods Market Inc. (WFM) New Position: September 2015

Whole Foods Market Inc. operates as a retailer of natural and organic foods. It currently has approximately 405 stores located in the United States, Canada, and the United Kingdom. This is one grocery store chain I have really started to appreciate as our nation wrestles with obesity and other health-related problems related to poor diets and unhealthy eating habits. Whole Foods Market's shares are down more than 50% since their peak in the fall of 2013. Although same-store sales for older stores have not been impressive, demand for new stores is high, which is good news for both the consumer and the owners of Whole Foods Market shares. Management has a goal of opening 1,200 stores nationwide, which would about triple today's count. There are some stocks that trade at high P/E ratios in comparison to their earnings growth rate and I have found Whole Foods Market to be such a stock. For example, over the last 10 years, Whole Foods Market's average annual P/E ratio was 36.2 and over the last five years it was 34.8. In such situations, I will usually resort to the P/E ratio to determine my purchase price. Analysts also estimate that Whole Foods Market's long-term EPS growth rate will be about 13.4%, and that the company will earn $1.68 per share for the 2015 year. Whole Foods Market also is debt-free. Using Whole Foods Market's average annual P/E ratio of 34.8, which is the lower of the two long-term P/E ratios, gives me a stock trading price of $58.46. I paid an average price of $31.96 per share for this initial purchase. If the stock performs as it has in the past, then my margin of safety for this purchase is about 45%.

PayPal Holdings Inc. (PYPL) Increased Position: September 2015

Mr. Elfenbein originally set the buy below price to $42 per share for PayPal Holdings. During my last check of his buy list, he had adjusted his buy below price to $38.00. I paid an average price of $32.86 per share for this purchase.

Freeport-McMoRan Inc. (FCX) Increased Position: September 2015

I paid an average price of $9.67 per share for this purchase.

Apple Inc. (AAPL) New Position: October 2015

I have lost money on most of my investments into technology companies and have become hesitant about investing in companies that fall within the technology industry; however, I had looked at Apple Inc. for several years and I think that the company is one of the world's best innovators, if it isn't the best. Apple Inc. also is currently the world's largest company with a market capitalization that currently stands at more than $620 billion. What's even more impressive is that it currently has more than $150 billion in cash and no debt. Apple has grown it's EPS at an annual rate of more than 37% for the last five years, and analysts estimate it will grow it EPS at a long-term rate of 14.7%. Apple's five-year average return on equity stands at 37% and its five-year average return on capital stands at 40%. In November 2014, I estimated Apple to have a fair value of $143.26 to $150.80 per share based on estimated earnings of $7.54 for the 2014 year. Analysts are estimating EPS for the 2015 year to be $9.13 per share. I decided not to even bother performing a new estimate of Apple's fair value and just based my decision to purchase shares on my 2014 fair value estimates. I paid an average price of $110.89 per share for this purchase based on 2014 estimates and my margin of safety is still about 23% to 26% for this stock.

eBay Inc. (EBAY) Increased Position: October 2015

I paid an average of $23.96 per share for this purchase.

Whole Foods Market Inc. (WFM) Increased Position: October 2015

I paid an average price of $33.33 per share for this purchase.

International Business Machines Corp. (IBM) New Position: October 2015

I have been watching IBM for a long time and felt that now was the right time to purchase some of its shares since the stock is currently down more than 19% from its 52-week high. Like Apple Inc., IBM is one of the world's greatest innovators when it comes to technology. I obtained the financial information for IBM from a Jan. 2, 2015, report provided by *The Value Line*

Investment Survey. The Value Line Investment Survey is second to none when it comes to the financial services and information that it provides to its subscribers and at very reasonable costs for all that the subscribers are getting. Looking at the report prepared on IBM, I found that IBM had managed to grow its EPS at an annual rate of 14% over the past five years, and at an annual rate of 13% over the past 10 years. IBM also had a long-term average return on equity of 36% and a long-term average return on capital of 18%. Net profit margins also have increased over the long term, growing from an annual rate of 9% in 2004 to an annual rate of 16% in 2014. The report provides projections of the trading price for IBM stock for the 2017 to 2019 years, and projects that the shares will trade at a low of $220 and a high of $270 per share. If shares trade in the projected price range, the annual total return would be 10-16% based on IBM's closing price of $161.44 at the time the report was prepared. I purchased these initial shares of IBM at an average price of $149.79 per share.

eBay Inc. (EBAY) Increased Position: October 2015
I paid an average of $24.58 per share for this purchase.

International Business Machines Corp. (IBM) Increased Position: October 2015
I purchased these shares of IBM at an average price of $150.16 per share.

Keurig Green Mountain Inc. (GMCR) Increased Position: October 2015
I paid an average price of $51.80 per share for this purchase.

Apple Inc. (AAPL) Increased Position: October 2015
Legendary investor Carl Icahn has said he believes the shares are worth $240 each, but many analysts are in disagreement with him concerning his estimate and they believes the shares are not worth nearly as much. I believe the shares are worth much more than their current trading price. I paid an average price of $115.33 per share for this purchase.

Valeant Pharmaceuticals International Inc. (VRX) New Purchase: October 2015

My purchase of Valeant Pharmaceuticals is a coattail purchase. From my research of the business, it's a very impressive one that has great growth opportunities. The stock is down more than 56% from its 52-weeks high of $263.81. It has been beaten down as the result of some bad news about the company, but the fact is that the information is not going to cripple such an amazing business. It's going to take some time, but I think that it will eventually recover. Lou Simpson, Leon Cooperman and Bill Ackman are master investors who currently own shares of the stock, and their ownership sparked my interest in owning shares. The best part is that I paid much less for these shares than they did. I paid an average price of $115.66 per share for this purchase.

EBay Inc. (EBAY) Sold Out: November 2015

My initial purchase of eBay Inc. was in October 2014, and the purchase was a coattail investment. At the time, I found that many of the pros had been loading up on its shares. Seth Klarman, Wallace Weitz, Carl Icahn, Joel Greenblatt, George Soros and Ken Fisher are just a few of the investors that were buying shares at the time. I must admit, the one investor that had the biggest impact on my decision to go ahead and purchase shares of eBay Inc. was Carl Icahn, whom many consider to be a more successful investor than Warren Buffett. With a recent check of GuruFocus.com, I found Mr. Icahn had sold out his position in eBay Inc. It's my belief that he was mainly after the PayPal Holdings Inc. shares that resulted from the spin-off that holders of eBay shares received. Since this was a coattail purchase, I decided to also sell my shares of eBay Inc. and continue to hold onto my PayPal shares. I paid an average price of $22.56 per share for my eBay shares and sold them at an average price of $28.56 per share. My total return from this sell was 26.6% and my annual rate of return was 44.4%.

PRA Group Inc. (PRAA) Increased Position: November 2015

I paid an average price of $37.15 per share for this purchase. At the time of this purchase, the shares were down almost 37% in comparison to my previous purchase.

Freeport-McMoRan Inc. (FCX) Increased Position: November 2015

I was able to purchase these shares for the average cost of $8.57 per share.

Keurig Green Mountain Inc. (GMCR) Increased Position: November 2015

I paid an average price of $40.47 per share for this purchase.

Whole Foods Market Inc. (WFM) Increased Position: November 2015

I paid an average price of $30.41 per share for this purchase.

International Business Machines Corp. (IBM) Increased Position: November 2015

I purchased these shares of IBM at an average price of $139.70 per share.

Joy Global Inc. (JOY) Increased Position: November 2015

I had not purchased shares of Joy Global since January 2014, but shares have fallen more than two-thirds in price since then. I think that the shares were a real bargain in January 2014, and at my purchase price of $15.26 per share for these shares, I think that they are a steal.

TransGlobe Energy Co. (TGA) Increased Position: November 2015

Shares have fallen significantly since my last purchase of this stock. I paid $2.18 per share for this purchase and I'm convinced a rebound in the energy market will result in the stock becoming a multi-bagger.

Valeant Pharmaceuticals International Inc. (VRX) Increased Position: November 2015

This is my second purchase of shares of Valeant Pharmaceuticals. Shares have fallen about 40% since my last purchase, which makes these shares much more attractive for me. I paid an average price of $69.93 per share for this purchase.

Keurig Green Mountain Inc. (GMCR) Sold Out: December 2015

I begin building this positioning in Keurig Green Mountain Inc. in August 2015 and added to the position in October and November. On Dec. 4, shares of Keurig Green Mountain soared more than 72% after the announcement that it would be taken private in a $92 per share, or $13.9 billion, buyout by JAB Holding Co. I don't usually hold on to my shares once the share price is trading near the buyout price, and decided not to do so this time either. My average cost per share was $49.93 and my selling price was $89.55 per share. My total return from this sale was a gain of 79.3% and my annual rate of return from this sale was an amazing 1019.6% because the shares were held for such a short period of time.

Apple Inc. (AAPL) Increased Position: December 2015

I paid an average price of $112.45 for this purchaser.

Whole Foods Market Inc. (WFM) Increased Position: December 2015

I paid an average price of $33.62 per share for this purchase.

Valeant Pharmaceuticals International Inc. (VRX) Increased Position: December 2015

Shares have reversed in price since my last purchase and have increased 56% since my last purchase. I paid an average price of $69.93 per share during my purchase in November and this purchase cost me $109.12 per share.

International Business Machines Corp. (IBM) Increased Position: December 2015

I purchased these shares of IBM at an average price of $138.90 per share.

PRA Group Inc. (PRAA) Increased Position: December 2015

I paid an average price of $37.63 per share for this purchase.

Anika Therapeutics Inc. (ANIK) Increased Position: December 2015

I purchased these shares at an average price of $38.08 per share.

Orbital ATK Inc. (OA) Sold Out: January 2016

As the stock market begin to drop because of the significant drop in the price of crude oil, I begin to use my cash reserve to add to my favorite positions within my portfolio. Before I knew it, I had literally spent almost all of my cash reserve on stocks. After my spending spree, things got a lot worse, and stocks I purchased or already owned in my portfolios got even cheaper, knocking both of my portfolios down about 25%. The swift and sudden drop really surprised me. With a desire to continue to add to my positions in the future, I sold Orbital ATK to begin rebuilding my cash position. My main reason for the sale of Orbital ATK was that it was one of the few stocks in the portfolio showing a profit; and of those showing a profit, it was my least favorite. Now, what I have just revealed to you definitely is the wrong way to go about rebuilding my cash reserve. The fact is that I should never have used most of it up in the first place. Even so, with stocks now beaten down to such low prices, I will continue to add to other positions within my portfolio for my favorite stocks when the funds are available. I paid an average price of $74.81 per share for my Orbital ATK shares and sold the shares at an average price of $84.19 per share. My total return from this sale was a gain of 12.5% and my annual rate of return from this sale was 17.1%.

Valeant Pharmaceuticals International Inc. (VRX) Increased Position: January 2016

I paid an average price of $92.46 per share for this purchase.

Chicago Bridge & Iron Co. (CBI) Increased Position: January 2016

Had I been as patient with my purchases of other stocks as I've been when building my position in Chicago Bridge & Iron Co., my portfolio would definitely be in much better shape. Again, the company's story has not changed. I paid an average price of $34.00 per share for this purchase compared to an average price of $46.94 for my last purchase. As you can see, the shares have fallen considerably in price.

PayPal Holdings Inc. (PYPL) Increased Position: January 2016

I still have not attempted to determine the intrinsic value of the PayPal Holdings stock shares, but paid an average price of $31.93 per share during this purchase.

Freeport-McMoRan Inc. (FCX) Increased Position: January 2016

For this purchase, I paid an average price of $4.00 per share, which means that this stock has fallen more than 50% since my last purchase.

Coach Inc. (COH) Sold Out: February 2016

My average cost for my total share purchases for this position was $36.44 per share. I really like this company but decided to sell in order to purchase shares in other companies within my portfolio that are trading at a much larger discount to their intrinsic value such as Chicago Bridge & Iron Co. and PRA Group Inc. I also own shares of Michaels Kors Holdings Ltd., and I believe it and Coach Inc. are so similar that what affects one will generally affect the other. I also believe that Michael Kors Holdings is currently the better of the two companies, but it's my intention to sell out that position too, so I can continue to add to other positions I currently own that I think offer a much better value. My average selling price for Coach Inc. was $36.30 per share. I lost about .14 cents per share when I sold out this position. In other words, I lost very little money, but the reality is that I actually came out ahead and ended with a capital gain of $273.97 because of dividends that were received. My total return from this sale was a gain of 3.2% and my annual rate of return from this sale was 3.4%. I received a total of $293.00 in dividends during my ownership of Coach Inc.

EZCORP Inc. (EZPW) Increased Position: February 2016

I had not added to this position since August 2014. At that time, I paid an average cost of $9.70 per share for EZCORP. The share price has fallen off a cliff since my last purchase and I purchased these shares at an average cost of $2.81 per share.

Freeport-McMoRan Inc. (FCX) Increased Position: February 2016

I paid an average price of $7.00 per share for this purchase.

Atwood Oceanics Inc. (ATW) Increased Position: February 2016

It's amazing to believe that I paid more than $49.00 per share for my initial purchase of Atwood Oceanics Inc. This purchase cost me a whopping $6.59 per share and yet I'm still very happy owning the stock and will buy more shares at this low, low price.

Joy Global Inc. (JOY) Increased Position: February 2016

This purchase cost me $12.15 per share.

DXP Enterprises Inc. (DXPE) Increased Position: February 2016

I paid an average price of $14.04 per share for this purchase.

Michael Kors Holdings Ltd. (KORS) Sold Out: March 2016

My average purchase price was $54.53 per share and my selling price for Michael Kors Holdings Ltd. was $57.20 per share. My total return from this sale was a gain of 4.9% and my annual rate of return from this sale was 6.2%.

Apple Inc. (AAPL) Increased Position: March 2016

I paid an average price of $100.88 for this purchaser.

International Business Machines Corp. (IBM) Increased Position: March 2016

I purchased these shares of IBM at an average price of $135.04 per share.

Chicago Bridge & Iron Co. (CBI) Increased Position: March 2016

I paid an average price of $33.81 per share for this purchase.

DXP Enterprises Inc. (DXPE) Increased Position: March 2016

I paid an average price of $13.70 per share for this purchase.

Valeant Pharmaceuticals International Inc. (VRX) Increased Position: March 2016

I paid an average price of $66.21 per share for this purchase.

PRA Group Inc. (PRAA) Increased Position: March 2016

I paid an average price of $30.08 per share for this purchase.

Whole Foods Market Inc. (WFM) Increased Position: March 2016

I paid an average price of $33.62 per share for this purchase.

Joy Global Inc. (JOY) Increased Position: March 2016

I paid an average price of $15.70 per share for this purchase.

PayPal Holdings Inc. (PYPL) Reduced Position: May 2016

I decided to reduce my position in PayPal Holdings Inc. after I noticed that Seth Klarman, Carl Icahn, George Soros and a host of other pros had been reducing their positions in PayPal Holdings over the past several months. I sold only half of my shares, and decided to continue to hold onto the remaining shares for now. My cost basis for the PayPal Holdings shares was $30.93 per share and my average selling price was $39.21 per share. My total return from this sell was a gain of 26.8% and my annual rate of return from this sale was 35.3%.

United Therapeutics Corp. (UTHR) New Position: May 2016

United Therapeutics Corp. is a biotech company that really excites me when I look at its financial numbers. For the worry-free investor, it would appear to be the perfect stock. So, when shares fell from a high of $190 to my average buy price of $111.58 per share, it was just too good of a deal to pass up. United Therapeutics has managed to grow its EPS at an annual rate of almost 47% over the most recent five-year period. United Therapeutics also reported having more than $950 million in cash with almost no long-term debt. Its 2015 profit margin stood at more than 44% with a five-year average return on equity of 28%, and a five-year average return on capital of 25%.

Analysts estimate that United Therapeutics will earn $13.00 for the 2016 year and estimate a long-term EPS growth rate of 11.5%. I estimated United Therapeutics to have a fair value of $149.50 to $191.75 per share. I paid an average price of $111.58 per share for this purchase, which gives me a minimum margin of safety of 34.8% based on the lower figure of $149.50. Motley Fool's Caps community has assigned the stock 5 stars out of 5.

Freeport-McMoRan Inc. (FCX) Reduced Position: July 2016

I decided to reduce my position in Freeport-McMoRan Inc. to rid the position of the more expensive shares and to use the money received from the sell to again build my cash position within the portfolio. Even with what appears to be a premature sell, my returns were not bad. My average cost for the shares that were sold was $9.94 per share and my selling price was $11.31 per share. The total return from the sell was 13.8% and the annual rate of return was 16.8%. I also want to mention that I sold only about 20% of the shares from my position because I really like this stock.

Whole Foods Market Inc. (WFM) Sold Out: July 2016

I decided to sell out of my position in Whole Foods Market Inc., although I'm convinced the company is a great long-term investment. At this time, my cash reserve is still relatively low in comparison to the account's total value and I'm also interested in continuing to build my position within United Therapeutics Corp. One of my sell rules is to sell a stock from my portfolio when a better and more favorable investment becomes available for purchase. Well, I think United Therapeutics is a much better long-term investment than Whole Foods Market. I didn't lose any money on this sell, but I didn't make much either. My average cost for Whole Foods Market was $32.67 per share and my average selling price was $32.80 per share. My total return from this sale was a gain of 0.5% and my annual rate of return from this sale was 0.8% The return calculations do not include $95.68 in dividends that were received in 2016.

United Therapeutics Corp. (UTHR) Increased Position: July 2016

I paid an average price of $110.05 per share for this purchase.

Joy Global Inc. (JOY) Sold Out: July 2016

It was not my intention to sell Joy Global anytime soon, but sometimes situations will arise that leave you with no better option. I learned on July 21 that Joy Global Inc. had agreed to be acquired by Komatsu Ltd. for $3.7 billion, or $28.30 per share. The deal is expected to close by the middle of 2017, meaning it will take almost a year for the acquisition to close. In response to the announcement shares moved from a low of $22.65 on July 20th to a high of $28.30 on July 21. So, as you can see, the shares have already moved to within the acquiring price range. My initial purchase cost me $59.82 per share, but as the stock continued to fall in price over the last few years, I continued to add to my position. My average cost per share for Joy Global was $27.20 and my selling price was $27.95 per share. So, I didn't make much money but I'm glad I didn't lose any either. My total return from this sale was a gain of 3.1% and my annual rate of return from this sale was 2.3%. These figures include dividend income of $174.61 that was received during my ownership of these shares. Last, I want to mention that Komatsu Ltd. knows that it has gotten an excellent deal with its agreement to purchase Joy Global for such a low price. I know that the company is worth at least twice that amount but probably much more.

Air Methods Corp. (AIRM) New Position: July 2016

Air Methods Corp. is a provider of air medical emergency transport services and systems throughout the United States. It also designs, manufactures and installs medical aircraft interiors and other aerospace and medical transport products for domestic and international customers. Air Methods Corp. has managed to grow it EPS at an annual rate of almost 19% over the most recent five-year period. It has also managed to grow its book value at an annual rate of about 19% over the last seven to 10 years. Its five-year average return on equity is 22% and its five-year average return on capital is about 12%. Analysts estimate that Air Methods Corp. will grow its EPS at a long-term rate of 20%, but I wasn't as optimistic with my EPS estimate and assigned a lower long-term rate of 17%. For 2016, Air Methods Corp. is expected to earn $3.52 per share. I estimate Air Methods Corp. has a fair value of $54.43 to $56.38 per share. I bought these initial shares at an average price of $33.65 per share. Motley Fool's Caps community has assigned the stock 4 stars out of a possible 5 stars.

United Therapeutics Corp. (UTHR) Increased Position: August 2016
I paid an average price of $125.86 per share for this purchase.

BofI Holding Inc. (BOFI) New Position: August 2016
I have been hesitant about investing my money into banking and financial stocks since the financial crisis struck in 2008 because some of my biggest investment losses were from banking and financial stocks I owned at the time. Fast forward into 2016, and I have found a banking stock I really like that has produced some impressive numbers and has done so for several years now. The bank that I'm talking about is BofI Holding Inc. BofI Holding acts as the holding company for BofI Federal Bank, which provides consumer and business banking products to customers in the United States through the internet. According to a Motley Fool report, during the first quarter of 2016, BofI Holding's net income grew by 70% from a year ago, its earnings per share grew by 65%, and its total assets grew by 40%, which includes a 38% growth in deposits. The stock's price has been beaten down by short-sellers because of several allegations that were made against the bank in 2015. As of now, none of the allegations has been proven. Yet, the stock is down about 50% from its 52-week high. BofI Holding has managed to grow it EPS at an annual rate of 19% over the most recent five-year period. It has also managed to grow its book value at an annual rate of 17% over the last 7-10 years. Its five-year average return on equity is 17% and its five-year average return on assets is 1.4%. I learned that it's best to use return on assets instead of return on capital when analyzing banks and other financial institutions, and that the investor should look for a return on assets of 1 or greater. Analysts estimate BofI Holding will grow its EPS at a long-term rate of 10%; however, I was a little more optimistic with my EPS estimate, and assigned a higher long-term rate of 14%. For 2016, BofI Holding is expected to earn $1.78 per share. I estimate BofI Holding has a fair value of $27.60 to $31.17 per share. I bought

these initial shares at an average price of $18.14 per share. Motley Fool's Caps community has assigned the stock 5 stars (out of 5).

PayPal Holdings Inc. (PYPL) Sold Out: August 2016

I decided now is probably a good time to sell out my remaining position in PayPal Holdings Inc. I sold 50% of my shares in May 2016 at a higher price. During a review of my portfolio in July 2016, I found that Seth Klarman, Carl Icahn, George Soros and several other pros were once again reducing their positions of PayPal Holdings Inc. Since this stock was a coattail purchase, I simply wanted to continue to mimic their actions. My cost for these PayPal Holdings shares was $32.35 per share and my average selling price was $37.14 per share. My total return from this sell was a gain of 14.8% and my annual rate of return from this sale was 19.1%.

Air Methods Corp. (AIRM) Increased Position: August 2016

I paid an average price of $35.48 per share for this purchase.

PRA Group Inc. (PRAA) Increased Position: September 2016

I paid an average price of $31.73 per share for this purchase.

Chicago Bridge & Iron Co. (CBI) Increased Position: September 2016

I paid an average price of $28.99 per share for this purchase.

Valeant Pharmaceuticals International Inc. (VRX) Increased Position: September 2016

I purchased my initial shares of Valeant Pharmaceuticals in October 2015 as a coattail purchase. Great investors such as Wallace Weitz, Bill Ackman, Lou Simpson, Ruane Cunniff and Leon Cooperman owned significant positions of Valeant Pharmaceuticals stock shares at the time, and I was excited to actually be able to purchase Valeant Pharmaceuticals shares at a much lower price than most of them had paid. My initial shares cost me $115.66 per share and this purchase cost me $28.17 per share. Oh my! How the mighty has fallen! I'm standing at a significant loss at this time, but believe that because of the great amount of influence or pressure from the likes of Bill Ackman and other great investors with significant holdings of Valeant's stock shares, management will get things turned around and headed in the right direction. If they don't, they will be replaced by someone who can. No doubt, it's going to take some time and effort to turn this company around, but I believe that it will be fixed and it's my plan to hold on to my Valeant stock shares until it does. Of course, I expect that the shares will probably fall even further before a turnaround is seen.

United Therapeutics Corp. (UTHR) Increased Position: September 2016

I paid an average price of $121.88 per share for this purchase.

DXP Enterprises Inc. (DXPE) Sold Out: September 2016

I paid $41.61 per share for my initial purchase of DXP Enterprises and the shares traded as low as $12.67 per share during my holding period. As I continued to add to my position in DXP Enterprises at much lower prices than my initial cost, my average cost per share dropped with each purchase leaving me with an average cost of $25.04 per share for my share purchases.

I decided to sell DXP Enterprises in an effort to better diversify my portfolio since DXP Enterprises' revenue is greatly affected by the oil and gas and the commodities industries because DXP Enterprises provides a variety of services and equipment to them. Since the portfolio already had three other stocks in it that were in the energy sector, I thought that now would be a good time to jettison this position and use the funds from the sell to continue to add newer positions to the portfolio when they become available at the right price. DXP Enterprises debt/equity ratio reached 1.76, which was the highest it had been since my ownership of the stock. My average cost per share for DXP Enterprises was $25.04 and my selling price was $26.96 per share. My total return from this sale was a gain of 7.7% and my annual rate of return from this sale was 6.7%.

Air Methods Corp. (AIRM) Increased Position: September 2016

I paid an average price of $31.45 per share for this purchase.

International Business Machines Corp. (IBM) Increased Position: September 2016

I paid an average price of $156.20 per share for this purchase.

BofI Holding Inc. (BOFI) Increased Position: September 2016

I paid an average price of $22.28 per share for this purchase.

EZCORP Inc. (EZPW) Sold Out: October 2016

I initially purchased shares of EZCORP Inc. in May 2012 at an average cost of $23.99 per share, which means I held this position for about four years and five months. Holding on to my shares for this length of time easily met Philip A. Fisher's three-year rule. During my ownership, the stock fell as low as $2.44 per share. I last added to my position in February 2016. At that time, I said that the share price had fallen off a cliff because the shares were trading in the upper-$2-per-share price range, and I made my final purchase at an average cost of $2.81 per share. Since that time, the share price has increased by more than 278%. Although I think EZCORP Inc. will work out well as a long-term holding, I still decided to sell my shares at this time. My average cost per share for EZCORP Inc. was $10.18 and my selling price was $10.66 per share. My total return from this sale was a gain of 4.7% and my annual rate of return from this sale was 1.4% or slightly higher.

International Business Machines Corp. (IBM) Sold Out: November 2016

I purchased my initial shares of IBM in October 2015 and mentioned then that IBM is one of the world's greatest innovators when it comes to technology, and my view of IBM has not changed. I purchased IBM with the intention of holding the shares until I earned a total return of 50%, which I thought was possible within three years of my initial purchase. IBM is what Peter Lynch would refer to as a "stalwart." Stalwarts are companies with large market capitalization whose growth has slowed, but they are capable of providing steady and predictable returns. Stalwarts also tend to pay dividends. So, I think that IBM stock is still an excellent investment to own. One of my rules for selling a specific stock is when I have found what I believe to be a better option in which to invest my funds and that's exactly my reason for selling these shares. I would never attempt to time the stock market because I know I can't and would only fail while trying to do so. What's interesting, though, is the fact that several of my favorite stocks currently seem to be hitting 52-week lows at about the same time. These are stocks that I have been watching for several years but would not purchase because I estimated them to be too expensive. I'm not going to jump in and start buying right now because I want to wait and see if they are going to get even cheaper. My average cost per share for IBM Corp. was $144.83 and my selling price was $152.39 per share. My total return from this sale was a gain of 8.0% and my annual rate of return was 9.7%, which includes $248.70 in dividends that were received.

Apple Inc. (AAPL) Sold Out: November 2016

There will be times when you will probably find yourself selling a stock prematurely that you really like. For me, Apple Inc. is such a stock. I'm selling for the same reasons that I sold IBM Corp. My average cost for Apple Inc. was $110.67 per share and my selling price was $111.05 per share. My total return from this sale was a gain of 1.6% and my annual rate of return was 2.5%, which includes $175.27 in dividends that were received.

Freeport-McMoRan Inc. (FCX) Sold Out: December 2016

I sold out my position in Freeport-McMoRan Inc., although I think we will see a dramatic increase in the stock's trading price over the next few years. I have made a good profit from my investment, so I won't complain when it happens. My average cost for these shares was $6.49 per share and my selling price was $14.79 per share. My total return from this sale was a gain of 128.3% and my annual rate of return was 143.6%, which also includes $25.35 in dividends that were received.

Air Methods Corp. (AIRM) Sold Out: December 2016

I actually took a loss on these shares, which has become a very rare thing for me to do. I paid an average price of $34.22 per share for these shares and sold them at an average price of $31.57 per share. My total return from this sell was a loss of -7.7% and my annual rate of return was -22.4%.

BofI Holding Inc. (BOFI) Sold Out: December 2016

BofI Holding has really taken off in the short time period I held the shares in my account. With the sale of these shares, my cash position is currently more than 50% of my account balance and the largest cash position that I have ever held in the account. My average cost for BofI Holding Inc. was $20 per share and my selling price was $26.89 per share. My total return from this sale was a gain of 34.4% and my annual rate of return was 170.5%.

United Therapeutics Corp. (UTHR) Increased Position: December 2016

I paid an average price of $142.02 per share for this purchase. These shares traded as low as $97.52 on June 27 of this year, which means the shares are up more than 45% since then.

PRA Group Inc. (PRAA) Sold Out: February 2017

I initially bought shares of PRA Group a little more than two years ago at an average price of $52.85 per share. During my ownership, I managed to buy shares as low as $29.88 per share. The shares traded as low as $20 per share in February 2016. My average cost for PRA Group shares was $41.90 and my selling price was $$41.62. My total return from the sale was a loss of -0.6% and my annual rate of return was a loss of -0.4%. The same day I sold my shares at the small loss, the shares closed at $42.15 per share and reached a high of $42.25 per share. It had been a year and three months since the shares traded in that price range. The stock market does have a since of humor, doesn't it?

Atwood Oceanics Inc. (ATW) Increased Position: February 2017

I paid an average price of $10.24 per share for this purchase.

United Therapeutics Corp. (UTHR) Sold Out: February 2017

I paid an average price of $125.26 per share for United Therapeutics Corp. and sold the shares at an average price of $154.76 per share. My shares were sold as the result of the stop-loss that I was experimenting with using only these shares and Anika Therapeutics Inc. shares. The day before selling United Therapeutics Corp., the stock closed at $167.92 per share; and the day of my sell, the stock closed at $146.98, or closed down about 12.5%. My total return from this sell was a gain of 23.5% and my annual rate of return from this sell was 55.9%.

Anika Therapeutics Inc. (ANIK) Sold Out: February 2017

I paid an average price of $39.48 per share for Anika Therapeutics Inc. and sold my shares at an average price of $46.11 per share. My total return from this sell was a gain of 16.8% and my annual rate of return from this sell was 11.1%. As in the case of United Therapeutics Corp., these shares were sold as the result of the stop-loss that I had in place with them. After the experiment, I found that I don't really like the stop-loss, although it can be a very effective damage control tool.

TransGlobe Energy Co. (TGA) Increased Position: March 2017

I paid an average price of $1.69 per share for this purchase.

Chicago Bridge & Iron Co. (CBI) Increased Position: March 2017

I paid an average price of $32.26 per share for this purchase.

Valeant Pharmaceuticals International Inc. (VRX) Increased Position: March 2017

I paid an average price of $13.16 per share for this purchase.

Icahn Enterprises LP (IEP) New Position: April 2017

Icahn Enterprises LP is an investment vehicle of legendary investor Carl Icahn. Mr. Icahn has been buying back shares of Icahn Enterprises LP for several years now, and paid more than $100 per share for some purchases that he made in 2014. I paid an average price of $48.13 per share for this purchase, which is less than half of what he paid for those shares in 2014.

Express Scripts Holding Co. (ESRX) New Position: April 2017

These shares have fallen more than 17% from their 52-week high of a little more than $80 per share. I paid an average price of $66.34 per share for this purchase.

Cognizant Technology Solutions Corp. (CTSH) New Position: April 2017

I have been watching Cognizant Technology Solutions' stock for many years and really like the stock. I made a big mistake when I failed to purchase shares of this stock during the Great Recession when they were really cheap. I paid an average price of $58.06 per share for this purchase.

Under Armour Inc. Class C (UA) New Position: April 2017

I decided to purchase this stock after seeing my supervisor, who is both a football coach and a track and field coach, was wearing a shirt, pants, jacket and sneakers together that were all Under Armour brand. I paid an average price of $17.60 per share for this purchase.

Tractor Supply Co. (TSCO) New Position: April 2017

I had been watching and waiting for the price of this stock to drop significantly for several years and now I think that it's current price is very attractive for the patient investor. I paid an average price of $65.54 per share for this purchase.

Fonar Corp. (FONR) New Position: May 2017

I found there were no analysts covering this particular company, although the stock has given investors a compound annual return of more than 52% over the last five years. I paid an average price of $19.59 per share for this purchase.

Dollar General Corp. (DG) New Position: May 2017

When I look at Dollar General Corp., I can't help but think that its stores are like baby Wal-Marts. Dollar General Corp. currently has a market capitalization of about $20 billion, and I think there's a lot more growth in store for it. I paid an average price of $72.65 per share for this purchase.

Biogen Inc. (BIIB) New Position: May 2017

Biogen Inc. is a biopharmaceutical company that develops, manufactures, and markets therapies for people living with serious neurological, autoimmune and rare diseases, such as leukemia, multiple sclerosis and Alzheimer's disease. I think the stock is cheap relative to what investors have been willing to pay for the shares in the past. The stock has traded at an average P/E of about 28 annually for the last five years and an average P/E of 24 annually for the last seven to 10 years. I paid an average of $260.72 per share for this purchase and analysts estimate Biogen Inc. will earn $22.57 per share next year. If the stock meets its EPS estimate and trades at the lower P/E of 24, then we can expect to see a trading price in the range of $541.68 next year. The stock may or may not approach this trading price, but one thing is for certain: at $260.72 per share, the stock is still a very good buy!

Bed Bath & Beyond Inc. (BBBY) New Position: May 2017

Bed Bath & Beyond is another stock that I had been watching for several years but would not purchase because I estimated it to be overvalued during most of that period. When Bed Bath & Beyond finally began trading in a price range that I felt was cheap, I was still hesitant about purchasing shares because of the fact that brick-and-mortar stores and mall based stores are currently in a serious retail slump resulting from the increasing dominance of online retailers, such as Amazon and eBay. While reading of a financial article, I learned that Kunar Kapoor, chief executive officer of Morningstar Inc., had said in a speech at his company's annual investment conference that there were only nine stocks in Morningstar's universe that had a rating of 5 stars. Please keep in mind that Morningstar's coverage universe consists of thousands of stocks; and yet out of those thousands of stocks, Bed Bath & Beyond was one of the only nine stocks that received Morningstar's highest rating of 5 stars. Knowing this gave me confidence to move forward with my purchase of shares. I paid an average price of $36.04 per share for this purchase.

F5 Networks Inc. (FFIV) New Position: May 2017

For a long time, I have been desiring to add a solid performing cybersecurity stock to my portfolio. After all, I believe the internet is currently the most important and most popular technological development in existence. Along with the popularity of the internet and cyberspace come the intent of using software or hardware to commit an assortment of internet crimes or to perform other acts that the public generally finds questionable. The truth is, things are only going to get worse and that will increase demand for security products and services from companies such as F5 Networks. F5 Networks is not a pure play cybersecurity stock, but it has a strong portfolio of security products and will no doubt take the necessary steps to continually strengthen its portfolio. F5 Networks also has an impressive track record when it comes to its EPS and had managed to increase its EPS every year for 14 consecutive years through 2016. I paid an average price of $131.03 per share for this purchase.

LKQ Corp. (LKQ) New Position: June 2017

LKQ Corp. is a leading provider of alternative and specialty parts to repair and accessorize automobiles and other vehicles. I paid an average price of $32.04 per share for this purchase.

Cognizant Technology Solutions Corp. (CTSH) Increased Position: June 2017

I paid an average price of $67.70 per share for this purchase.

Dollar General Corp. (DG) Increased Position: June 2017

I paid an average price of $70.50 per share for this purchase.

Express Scripts Holding Co. (ESRX) Increased Position: June 2017

I paid an average price of $65.69 per share for this purchase.

Icahn Enterprises LP (IEP) Increased Position: June 2017

I paid an average price of $50.61 per share for this purchase.

Tractor Supply Co. (TSCO) Increased Position: June 2017

I paid an average price of $52.90 per share for this purchase.

Under Armour Inc. Class C (UA) Increased Position: June 2017

I paid an average price of $19.69 per share for this purchase.

Bed Bath & Beyond Inc. (BBBY) Increased Position: June 2017

I paid an average price of $31.28 per share for this purchase.

T. Rowe Price Health Sciences Fund (PRHSX) New Position: July 2017

This fund is actual the first mutual fund I have purchased and owned within my portfolio, and that fact alone speaks volumes for the fund. The T. Rowe Price Health Sciences Fund invests in the health sciences sector, which includes health care services companies, pharmaceutical companies, biotechnology companies, and medical product and device providers. The fund seeks long-term capital appreciation and has done an excellent job for a very long time. Its returns are very impressive and are as follows: one-year, 15%; three-year, 12.1%; five-year, 20.4%; 10-year, 15.4%; and 15-year, 15.7% — and these returns are for a fund that is actively managed. Over the last 15 years, the total returns from this mutual fund are more than 700%, and the addition of the fund to my portfolio boosts the portfolio's exposure to the healthcare sector while also providing the portfolio with greater diversification. I paid an average price (net asset value) of $71.56 per share for this purchase.

Icahn Enterprises LP (IEP) Increased Position: July 2017

I paid an average price of $51.20 per share for this purchase.

Biogen Inc. (BIIB) Increased Position: July 2017

I paid an average price of $272.94 per share for this purchase.

F5 Networks Inc. (FFIV) Increased Position: July 2017

I paid an average price of $124.41 per share for this purchase.

Vanguard Consumer Staples ETF (VDC) New Position: July 2017

The Vanguard Consumer Staples Index Fund is an exchange traded fund, and this is actually the first one I have owned. I added this fund to the portfolio to boost the portfolio's exposure to the consumer staples sector, which tends to be one of the most stable sectors regardless of whether or not the economy is thriving or in a full recession. In 2008, for example, the average mutual fund lost about 40%, whereas the Vanguard Consumer Staples ETF experienced a loss of 16.5% during the same period. The Vanguard Consumer Staples ETF returns are: one-year, 0.75%; three-year, 9.0%; five-year, 12.4%; and 10-year, 10.0%. I paid an average price/net asset value of $140.68 per share for this purchase.

Fonar Corp. (FONR) Increased Position: July 2017

These shares have really climbed and are up almost 54% in price since my last purchase. I paid $30.12 per share for this purchase. I was willing to pay the higher price because I think these shares are worth much more than even the much higher price that was paid for this purchase.

LKQ Corp. (LKQ) Increased Position: July 2017

I paid an average price of $32.99 per share for this purchase.

T. Rowe Price Health Sciences Fund (PRHSX) Increased Position: August 2017

I paid an average price *(net asset value)* of $69.66 per share for this purchase.

Icahn Enterprises LP (IEP) Increased Position: August 2017

I paid an average price of $51.10 per share for this purchase.

Vanguard Consumer Staples ETF (VDC) Increased Position: August 2017

I paid an average price/net asset value of $140.28 per share for this purchase.

Icahn Enterprises LP (IEP) Increased Position: September 2017

I paid an average price of $51.32 per share for this purchase.

Dollar General Corp. (DG) Increased Position: September 2017

I paid an average price of $71.44 per share for this purchase.

BofI Holding Inc. (BOFI) New Position: September 2017

I sold out my original BofI Holding position in December 2016 only to again buy shares of this exciting internet bank. I paid an average price of $26.00 per share for this purchase.

United Therapeutics Corp. (UTHR) New Position: September 2017

I sold out this position in February 2017 at an average price of $154.76 per share. I paid an average price of $121.25 per share for this purchase.

"Of the stocks that I buy, three months later I am happy with less than a quarter of them." —Peter Lynch

PART FOUR

THE UNTAMEABLE STOCK MARKET

WHAT DO WE REALLY KNOW?

(Written in January 2008)

As we entered the year 2008, I could not help but to reflect on the financial markets of 2007. The housing sectors began to ease into a recession in 2006 and entered into a full recession in 2007. We saw the stocks of homebuilders, building material suppliers, home improvement warehouses and about any stock related to the housing and construction sector plummet in price. Yet, many experts were still debating whether or not the economy had really entered into a recession. We also began to see volatility in the stock market that had not been present for several years with the Dow displaying swings of 100 points or more in some trading sessions. We witnessed the cost of energy skyrocket as oil soared past the $100-per-barrel mark for the first time in history, contributing to an already increased jump in inflation. In 2007, we saw Wall Street's biggest and most powerful financial institutions, such as Merrill Lynch, Bear Stearns and Citigroup, come forward to acknowledge they had lost or were expecting to lose billions of dollars as a result of the subprime mortgage crisis created through aggressive lending practices combined with very low interest rates (cheap money). Many of the once high-flying banking stocks lost 50% or more of their value. Some of the nation's largest mortgage lenders, such as Countrywide Financial, also have had to admit they were in serious financial trouble and have lost billions of dollars as a result of the subprime mortgages in which they were invested. When it seemed the news could not get any worse, we learned that millions of American families were in jeopardy of losing their homes, which were pushed on them through predatory lending practices. Home values also began dropping all over the United States, with many homeowners owing more on them than they were actually worth. Do you think most of the Wall Street experts saw all of this coming? No way!

Now, we have entered into 2008, and many financial experts are debating on whether or not the economy has entered a recession. Perhaps, a year from now, some will still be debating this matter. When I began to think of all that had transpired, it reinforced my belief that short-term investing is a big gamble that's hard to win. Gambling should be done in Las Vegas, not on the stock market. One thing is for sure in either situation, the house has the advantage. No investor should have to be stressed or worried about the investment decisions that he or she makes. So, when it comes to the stock market, what do we really know? We now know that nobody knows what the stock market is going to do next! Here's a thought, 10 years from now, the investors who think and invest long term are likely to be in much better shape within their portfolios than most other types of gamblers… I mean investors.

"The stock market is the story of cycles and the human behavior that is responsible for overreaction in both directions." —Seth Klarman

IT'S OFFICIAL

(Written Tuesday, Dec. 2, 2008)

Yes, it's official!!! According to the National Bureau of Economic Research, we are currently in a recession that began in December 2007. There is no doubt in my mind this current recession began a while back. One thing is for certain, most of Wall Street's experts as well as the rest of the world were caught off guard by this recession, which has been determined to be the most severe one since the Great Depression. Should you and I be worried? I don't think so. History has shown that in times in which there has been great pessimism concerning the economy, fortunes have been made. John Templeton proved this to be true by borrowing money to invest during the start of World War II. He was investing money in the stock market while everyone else was taking theirs out. According to research, he bought 100 shares of 104 that were trading for $1 or less per share, and 34 of the companies happened to be in bankruptcy. A few years later, he sold his investments, making a hefty profit in the process. That event started him on his way to what would be a long, prosperous and amazing career, and would establish him as a pioneer of value investing and global investing. I believe any time is the right time to invest in the right stocks at the right prices.

"You get recessions, you have stock market declines. If you don't understand that's going to happen, then you're not ready, you won't do well in the markets." —*Peter Lynch*

ONE FOR THE AGES

Some are calling the recession that began in 2007 the Great Recession because of its impact around the world. The year 2008 was easily the worst year for the global economy since the 1930s. With all the negative news we see almost daily, it would have been easy for most investors to fail to take advantage of the stock market's excellent buying opportunities that presented themselves. In 2008, we saw stocks trading at rock bottom prices, and I'm talking about prices that most investors did not think those stocks would ever see again. Not any single event led to all of the pessimism seen throughout the U.S. and the global economy. Let's just take a look at some of the events that took place here in the U.S. in 2008, and I won't even bother trying to list events that were taking place in other parts of the world. The events are not in chronological order.

1.   Countrywide Financial fails because of its huge portfolio of risky mortgages and is bought by Bank of America.

2.   Bear Stearns fails and is bought by JPMorgan Chase.

3.   Freddie Mac and Fannie Mae, which own or guarantee about 58% of the nation's mortgages, are nationalized by the government to prevent them from collapsing after sustaining billions of dollars in losses.

4.   Housing foreclosures skyrocket with millions of homeowners receiving foreclosure notices or are at risk of losing their homes.

5.   The stock market enters the worst bear market since the 1930s, and sheds about $7 trillion in value.

6. American Insurance Group gets into financial trouble and receives no less than $130 billion from the federal government to stay afloat.

7. Even Wachovia Bank, considered to be a very strong financial institution, gets into financial trouble because of a portfolio of bad mortgages it purchased. Regulators approved of its sale to Wells Fargo.

8. Lehman Brothers becomes insolvent and files for bankruptcy protection. Lehman Brothers' failure also catapults the world's economies into a tailspin.

9. The small investor is not immune from what's going on in the economy, and most owners of 401(k)'s see their accounts drop 30-50% in value, with the average portfolio losing more than 40% of its value.

10. The credit market freezes up, making it almost impossible for many businesses to carry out day-to-day basic operations without some intervention from the federal government. Small businesses were hit especially hard, with thousands of them going out of business.

11. America's Big Three automotive manufacturers acknowledge the recession has taken a toll on an already crippled industry, and tells Congress they will need billions of dollars in assistance if they are going to survive the crisis.

12. Some money market funds broke the buck by falling below their fixed value of $1 per share, which is a very uncommon event in the investment world. Of course, the federal government came to their rescue to keep things from getting any worse.

13. Oil peaks above $147 per barrel results in further havoc to an already badly wounded economy. The outrageous fuel costs took their toll on most American households that were already struggling just to make ends meet. Fuel at one point reached a national average of more than $4 per gallon.

14. Housing values collapsed, leaving many homeowners with mortgages that were much higher than the properties were worth. Many homeowners found themselves stuck between a rock and a hard place. Not knowing what to do, some owners simply threw in the towel and walked away from their properties.

15. In 2008, we saw the worst annual job losses since 1945, with more than 2.6 million jobs lost and a national unemployment rate above 7%. Although those numbers are terrible, some cities and states fared much worse. For example, the unemployment rate in Detroit, Michigan, reached a staggering 21%, as of December 2008.

I think I have provided enough information to paint a picture of just how bad things really got. I have found that once we have come through a storm, it's always easy to look back and say things were not as bad as they seemed. Well, I'm here to say, "Yes they were!" Would you believe that even with all the commotion going on, there was a voice out there saying, "Now is the time to buy stocks?" Many investors could not believe anyone would have the nerve to make such a foolish recommendation like that in such a beaten down economy. The voice went on to say, "Be fearful when others are greedy and greedy when others are fearful," but it didn't stop there. It also said something to the extent of, "I'm buying stocks for my personal account now." Whose voice was it? None other than the voice of the amazing Warren Buffett. I'm convinced those who have been obedient to Mr. Buffett's recommendations will look back one day and be glad that they were.

"To come out ahead, you don't have to be right all the time, or even the majority of the time." —Peter Lynch

2015 IN REVIEW

When I consider the stock market's performance in 2015, I think that the market caused most investors to be fearful when they probably should have been greedy. No doubt, most investors find it very hard to be greedy in a volatile stock market that seems to have exploded in their faces (both U.S. and global markets). In the United States, economists and other financial experts were reassuring us the U.S. economy was still improving — albeit slowly — but the stock market seemed to have been telling us a totally different story. For example, the stock market climbed to new highs in May 2015, and then, in a quick reversal, dropped more than 10% by August of that year. In the end, the S&P 500 and the Dow ended the year with negative returns, which had not happened since the close of 2008. The S&P 500 lost 0.73%, but with the inclusion of dividends, it gained 1.38%.

I think that the biggest culprit to the market's lackluster performance was the significant drop in crude oil prices, which ended the year down more than 30%. Unfortunately, the energy sector's poor performance probably reflected in the portfolios of most individual investors, including me, with many of those portfolios significantly underperforming the stock market. What's really amazing is that many stocks fell to price levels below those they experienced during the Great Recession, and I'm speaking from experience because my Personal Worry-Free Stock Portfolio has been hammered, although my actively managed Traditional IRA held up well through 2015. Next, I'm going to talk about both of those portfolios and their performance, and whatever else comes to mind as I write.

Let's look first at my Personal Worry-Free Stock Portfolio. At the time of this writing, the portfolio is seven years and four months old. Although this portfolio is the older of my two portfolios, it has been my intention up to this point to be as passive as possible in the management of this portfolio, and to perform no sells from the portfolio unless absolutely necessary. I felt that if I could adhere to that rule with this portfolio, it would teach me much and would help me to produce a more informative book. Hopefully, my small sacrifice of sticking to that rule even when I don't want to will greatly benefit you as an investor too, since there is much that we can learn from using a disciplined approach to investing over long periods of time.

Now, let's see how things fared with the portfolio through the end of 2015. First, I want to mention that I entered 2015 with too much of the portfolio in cash. Even worse, I had held this large cash position within the portfolio for the last few years and had not really thought about it. I now admit that I should have put a large portion of the cash reserve to work sooner. I performed no sells from the portfolio in 2014 or 2015, but I did add two new positions to the portfolio in 2015. I bought both Chicago Bridge & Iron Co. and Anika Therapeutics Inc. in March 2015. Let me throw some numbers at you. The portfolio's total return at the end of 2014 was 131.8%, with an ending balance of $111,471.35. The portfolio's total return at the end of 2015 was 84.6%, with an ending balance of $88,743.79. I have not provided any annual rate of return figures because the software that I'm using is definitely producing figures that I know are not accurate. So, I decided to just look at the total return figures for this specific portfolio. The figures were calculated from the portfolio's inception date through the end of 2015, but dividends are not included in the calculations. In 2015 alone, the portfolio ended the year down 20.4%, and it seems that the carnage will continue in 2016. Still, as I mentioned earlier, the significant drop in crude oil prices is what has led to the stock market's drastic and swift decline also dragging stock prices way down in the process. Let me give you a few examples of what I'm talking about using a few of the stocks in the portfolio. In March 2012, Coach Inc. traded as high as $79.42 per share; and at the close of 2015, it traded for $32.73 per share. In April 2011, Joy Global Inc. traded as high as $103.44 per share; and at the close of 2015, it traded for $12.61 per share. In December 2013, DXP Enterprises Inc. traded for $116.88 per share; and at the close of 2015, it traded for $22.80 per share. Again, the poor performances of these stocks are mostly the result of the beaten down price of crude oil. Are there any lessons to be learned from this portfolio so far? Of course there are! I have listed them next.

- Never buy and hold (to the point of forgetting). Individual stocks are to be bought and actively managed.
- If you are not interested in actively managing your portfolio, stick to index funds and exchange traded funds, and you are still likely to outperform 90% of those invested in the stock market.
- The stock market can do some crazy things sometimes and the investors who realize that will be better prepared when it happens.
- When a stock becomes overvalued according to the metrics that you are using, consider reducing you position or selling the stock. If the stock is fairly valued, I would continue to hold it until a better opportunity presents itself. Just think about my huge loss of the gains I had earned with DXP Enterprises.
- Keep your portfolio concentrated, but make sure that it is properly diversified. For instance, with this portfolio, at least five stocks were greatly impacted by the price of oil. That was not my intention, and it resulted in significant losses for me with this portfolio.
- Invest for the long term but don't expect to hold every stock long term.
- Even outstanding stocks that are undervalued can fall to ridiculously low prices that leave the investor scratching his head.
- Finally, remember that the time to be buying stocks is in a beaten down stock market, such as the one we are currently experiencing in 2016, which carried over from 2015 as a result of the drop in the price of crude oil.

We will look next at my Traditional IRA. I decided I won't say too much about it since I said so much about my Personal Worry-Free Stock Portfolio. My Traditional IRA is the newer portfolio and I'm actively managing it in an attempt to maximize my returns from my investments. The portfolio was started in May 2012, and the cost basis of the original investments in this portfolio is $58,841.99. At the close of 2014, the portfolio had an ending balance of $110,341.96 and a total return of 87.5% with dividends reinvested. At the close of 2015, the portfolio had an ending balance of $109,331.91 and a total return of 85.8%. This portfolio lost less than 1% of its value through the rough-and-tumble 2015 year, and not losing a lot of money in the market is the key to building wealth.

"Building long-term wealth is like driving an automobile. If you narrowly focus on the stretch of road a few feet in front of your car, you risk making unnecessary adjustments and over steering. Only when you lift your eyes to focus further down the highway will you successfully reach your destination." —Christopher C. Davis

2016 IN REVIEW

It was not my intention to do a review of 2016, but since my Personal Worry-Free Stock Portfolio was down so much in 2015, I felt it was necessary to redeem myself. After all, I had no business writing a book on investing if I'm not practicing what I preach.

2016 got off to a rocky start with the stock market falling 10% in the first two weeks of the year, but was again in positive territory by the end of March. In June, the United Kingdom voted to leave the Eurozone, which many experts were predicting would send shockwaves throughout the world's markets, but it did not happen. So, be weary of stock market predictions. They are usually wrong. China's slowing economy was a major concern for the markets since China is now the world's second largest economy, although China's lackluster growth had carried over from 2015 and was nothing new. On Nov. 8, Donald Trump was elected President of the United States, and his election immediately contributed to investors' confidence with major indices rising 6% to 12% by the end of the year. In early 2016, oil reached a 13-year low, only to rebound with crude oil rising almost 45% in 2016, resulting in the energy sector being the year's best performing sector. On average, stocks of energy producers jumped 24% in 2016. At this time, crude oil is trading above $50 per barrel after trading as low as $25 per barrel in early 2016, and OPEC has also announced that it will reduce output in 2017 in an effort to push up the price of crude oil.

2016 was a very good year for small company stocks, as measured by the Wilshire U.S. Small-Cap Index, which had a total gain of 22.4% for the year. U.S. markets also hit record highs in the post-election rally, with the Dow Jones Industrial Average closing out the year at 19,762.60 on Dec. 30, with a total gain of 13.4% for the year. The S&P 500 finished the year with a total gain of 9.50% and the NASDAQ finished the year with a total gain of 7.50%.

Let's look now at the performance of my portfolios and see how they have fared in 2016. We will look first at my Personal Worry-Free Stock Portfolio, which is now eight years and four months old. Remember, I have intentionally been a passive investor when it comes to this particular portfolio. With it, I have no intention to perform any buys or sell unless absolutely necessary. In 2015, I admitted that I entered the year with too much cash. My cash position stood at 9.9% of the portfolio's total value at the close of 2016. In 2016, there were no buys or sells from the portfolio, and the portfolio had a total return of 9.2% for the year, which means it closely matched the performance of the S&P 500 for the year. The total return figure for my portfolio does not include dividends. The total return for the portfolio since its inception stood at 101.6% at the end of 2016. After my completion of this book, I will actively manage this portfolio just as I am actively managing my Traditional IRA for maximum profits.

Let's look next at my Traditional IRA. At the close of 2015, the portfolio contained 21 stocks, and at the close of 2016, the portfolio contained only nine stocks. It has been intentional on my part to shrink the portfolio, so I could better manage it. For me, 21 stocks were too many to keep tabs on. I believe with fewer stocks, I can do a much better job managing each position in the portfolio. The portfolio ended 2015 with a total value of $109,331.91, and ended 2016 with a total value of $117,582.55 for a gain of $8250.64, or 7.5%, for the year. The returns for the portfolio include dividends that were reinvested. You can refer to the section of the book entitled "Recent Transactions: Buy and Sells" to look at every transaction that took place with this portfolio in 2016. I want to mention that this portfolio is currently about 50% in cash. It's the largest cash position ever held in my portfolios, but I have no suspicions of the market collapsing anytime soon or anything else. I'm carrying a large cash position because it is my intention to make some major changes in the portfolio at a later date. When? I really don't know yet.

"Investors operate with limited funds and limited intelligence: they do not need to know everything. As long as they understand something better than others, they have an edge." —George Soros

PART FIVE

WE'RE ALMOST DONE

WRAPPING IT UP!

In this section, I will tell you how to implement the worry-free investing process, so you can truly invest like a stock market pro. I realize you have been provided with a large amount of information to put into practice, and the purpose of this section is to make that process as easy to possible to implement. So, let's get started.

STEP ONE - If you don't already have one, open a Traditional IRA or a Roth IRA with a reputable online brokerage firm such as Ameritrade, E*TRADE, Charles Schwab, Merrill Lynch or Scottrade. Be sure you qualify for the account before opening it by checking with a financial planner or a financial advisor. Also, if you have a retirement account at work, make sure you contribute enough income to it to receive all matching contributions.

STEP TWO - Screen for stocks using one or more stock screeners, such as the ones found at Google Finance, Motley Fool, Finviz, or Yahoo! Finance. In the section entitled "The Stock Screener: An Investor's Best Friend" and in the Appendix, I have provided a variety of screens based on the strategies of different investors that you can use when screening for stocks. This should generate a list of stocks that need to be further studied, and those stocks that do not pass the stress test should be eliminated. The stocks need to meet all eight criteria that have been set forth in the stress test.

STEP THREE - After the stress test, you should be left with a much smaller list of stocks that are truly the cream of the crop — stocks that will generate great wealth over the long term, but will also let you sleep well at night. Of the stocks that are left, determine which ones are the best five picks based on the results of the stress test. You want to do this so that you can also begin to create a buy list that you will be able to refer to once you are ready begin to purchase stocks.

STEP FOUR - Next, determine your purchase price for those stocks by using the modified PEG ratio. Use next year's EPS estimate and multiply it by the stock's five-year earnings growth rate estimate, which gives you the stock's estimated fair value. Remember, we don't ever want to purchase a stock at its estimated fair value, but we want to purchase it when it is undervalued. So, refer back to the section entitled "Using the PEG Ratio to Find Bargain Stocks" to see how to value a stock and discount the stock for risk. For those large, mature companies that are not growing quickly anymore, use the P/E ratio to estimate their trading price and to determine the price that you will pay for shares. Regardless of what you may hear or believe, the P/E ratio is still an effective measure to use in determining what to pay when purchasing most stocks.

STEP FIVE - Purchase the stock or stocks you like that meet your desired purchase price, putting a minimum of $500 into each stock, thereby spreading the commission cost over several more shares, which reduces your average cost per share.

STEP SIX - Repeat the process each time $500 or more becomes available for investing. Before you know it, you will find that you have built an excellent portfolio of stocks.

STEP SEVEN - Sit back and get ready to make some money because you are now investing like a stock market pro.

Build a portfolio of 10-20 stocks, and sell a stock only when it makes sense to do so. Don't forget to check the Motley Fool's Caps rating for any stocks that you are interested in purchasing. I will only purchase stocks that are rated 3 or more stars by the Caps community. Also, go back and review the Twelve

Essential Principles of the Stock Market Pro to make sure that you understand them so you can effectively adhere to them.

"If you are shopping for common stocks, choose them the way you would buy groceries, not the way you would buy perfume." —Benjamin Graham

GOD AND WEALTH

As you know by now, this is not a religious book and I'm definitely not a religious person, but I'm a Christian. Most people who are not Christians fail to realize that Christianity is not a religion, but a way of life. Christians strive daily to be like Christ. Mature Christians don't mind telling others about Christ and all that He has done for them, but they will not try to force their beliefs on others, and neither will I. I felt that since God is such an important part of my life, it would be unjust of me to not address a little of what He has to say about wealth and success.

Did you know there's nothing wrong with being wealthy? It's not what you have that matters, but what matters most is what you do with what you have and how you act because of what you have. That's what is important to God. King Solomon was the richest man that ever lived, and it was God Himself who caused King Solomon to succeed and to become rich. Here is what the Holy Bible says about one meeting between God and Solomon in 1 Kings 3:11-13: *And God said to him, Because thou hast asked this thing, and hast not asked for thyself long life; neither hast asked riches for thyself, nor asked the life of thine enemies; but hast asked for thyself understanding to discern judgment; Behold, I have done according to thy words: I have given thee a wise and an understanding heart; so that there was none like thee before thee, neither after thee shall any arise like unto thee. And I have also given thee that which thou hast not asked, both riches, and honor: so that there shall not be any among the kings like unto thee all thy days.*

So, in those verses, we see that God blessed King Solomon and it's understood to this day that King Solomon is the richest man that ever lived, even richer than Bill Gates, Carlos Slim and Warren Buffett. We find many examples in the Holy Bible where God blessed men and women to succeed. Here are some other biblical people that God blessed with wealth and/or success: Abraham and his sons, Job, Samson, King Hezekiah, Daniel, King Josiah, Joshua, King David, Ruth and Naomi, and Esther. Those mentioned are just a few of many individuals written about in the Holy Bible that God blessed with success. If He was concerned about their success, wouldn't He also be concerned about yours and mine?

Why would the sovereign, awesome God be concerned about you and me? The answer is simple: He loves us more than we could ever imagine. The writings of John the Apostle make this very clear, especially the third chapter of John. Just think, when we succeed, we are able to use our resources to bring glory to His name and we are also able to use those resources to help others that sincerely need help. In John 13:34, we find Jesus speaking. There, he says: *A new commandment I give unto you, that ye love one another; as I have loved you, that ye also love one another.*

I have lived for a little while now and I have found that the best and most powerful things we humans have going for us is love for God and love for one another. With love, the impossible become the possible. With love, "I can't" becomes "I can." With love, "I won't" becomes "I will."

Here is some proof of the importance of relying on God for success. 1 Samuel 2: 7-8 says, *The Lord maketh rich: he bringeth low, and lifteth up. He raiseth up the poor out of the dust, and lifteth up the beggar from the dunghill, to set them among princes, and to make them inherit the throne of glory: for the pillars of the earth are the Lord's and He hath set the world upon them.*

Proverbs 10:22 says, *The blessing of the Lord, it maketh rich, and He addeth no sorrow with it.*

So, not only does God want us to be successful, He wants us to have joy and happiness with that success. You and I have seen all the examples of famous people that have great wealth, but are truly unhappy. They resort to drugs, alcohol, sex and other destructive practices in search of answers for the way they are feeling, but those methods are not the answer. Just look at all of the stars that have lost their lives to drug abuse, alcohol abuse, or both. These people had a great void or emptiness in their lives and they were simply trying to fill it. How could it have been filled? It is my belief as a Christian that the emptiness that they felt could only be filled by a personal relationship with Jesus, the Christ.

In John 10:10, Jesus spoke and said, *The thief cometh not, but for to steal, and to kill, and to destroy: I am come that they might have life, and that they might have it more abundantly.*

So, what is my main point in this section? It is this: as you strive to build great wealth using the principles and strategies set forth in this book, put your trust first and foremost in God, and know that He wants you to succeed; and to the greatest extent, He is responsible for all of our successes. Along with the success that you achieve, know also that He wants you to have a life full of joy that comes from you having a personal relationship with His Son.

"Happiness comes from spiritual wealth, not material wealth." —*John Templeton*

ACKNOWLEDGEMENTS

My sincere thanks to:
God the Father and my Lord Jesus Christ, who is gracious and merciful to all. If it were not for God's love, what would I do? He has truly been better to me than I could ever deserve.

Carrie Pattersenn, my sweet and unselfish mother, who taught me the importance of putting the needs of others before my own if I truly wanted to be blessed and to be a blessing.

The great investors who have made this book possible because they cared enough to willingly share their wisdom and knowledge about investing with the rest of us.

Karen Rodgers, the first editor of my manuscript, who not only gave me the inspiration and courage to complete my book, but also to make it better. She's a real pro and will do a great job for any author! www.critiqueyourbook.com and krodgers.editor@gmail.com.

Sarah Tincher of Upwork, a global freelancing platform. Sarah performed the final edit of my manuscript and does fantastic work. She can be contacted through the **Upwork** website.

Angie, a professional graphic designer that I found at Fiverr, the world's largest freelance services marketplace. She does amazing work and you are going to love her prices! She can be contacted at **pro_ebookcovers** at the Fiverr website. If you need an eBook cover or printed book cover, hire her.

Jason and Marina Anderson of Polgarus Studio. I discovered Polgarus Studio while surfing the web several years ago and decided to print the homepage and save it just in case I needed formatting services in the future. After researching several formatting services, I'm so glad that I kept the Polgarus homepage. Jason and Marina are truly a professional team that want their customers happy and will go far beyond what is expected of them. I will use them for my next book too. They can be contacted through their website at www.polgarusstudio.com.

APPENDIX

SCREENS FOR INVESTING LIKE A STOCK MARKET PRO

Note: These are screens that I created that I believe will identify stocks that have similar fundamentals to those picked by the individuals that I named the screens after. Of course, further research is still necessary once the stocks have been retrieved. You may also find that most screeners don't contain a "return on capital" search criteria. Use of the "return on equity" should suffice.

THE BUFFETT STOCK SCREEN
Country: USA
Market Capitalization: $2 billion or greater
EPS Growth Rate (Past 5 Years): 15% or greater
Debt/Equity Ratio: Less than 0.50
Return on Equity (Past 5 Years): 15% or greater
P/E Ratio: 20 or less
Profit Margins: 15% or greater

THE SLATER STOCK SCREEN
Country: USA
Market Capitalization: $50 million or greater
PEG Ratio: Less than 1
EPS Growth Rate (Past 5 Years): 15% or greater
Debt/Equity Ratio: 0.50 or less
Return on Capital (Past 5 Years): 20%
Operating Profit Margins: 5% or greater

INVESTOR EDUCATION WEBSITES

Bankrate.com

Cnbc.com/investing

Daveramsey.com

Finance.yahoo.com

Fool.com

Howthemarketworks.com

Investopedia.com

Investors.com

Marketwatch.com

Money.cnn.com

Money.msn.com

Morningstar.com

Nasdaq.com

Seekingalpha.com

Thestreet.com

Zacks.com

COATTAIL INVESTING WEBSITES

Insidermonkey.com

Gurufocus.com

Stockpickr.com

STOCKS REPORTS

Gurufocus.com

Morningstar.com

Zacks.com

THE AUTHOR'S READING LIST

A Random Walk Down Wall Street, Burton G. Malkiel

Beating the Street, Peter Lynch

Beyond The Zulu Principle, Jim Slater

Buffett Beyond Value, Prem C. Jain

Buffettology, Mary Buffett & David Clark

Charles Schwab's Guide to Financial Independence, Charles R. Schwab

Choose Stocks Wisely, Paul W. Allen

Common Sense on Mutual Funds, John C. Bogle

Common Stocks and Uncommon Profits, Philip A. Fisher & George Guidal

Debt Free For Life, David Bach

Fight for Your Money, David Bach

Finding the Next Starbucks, Michael Moe

Flipping Burgers To Flipping Millions, Bernard Kelly

Jim Cramer's Get Rich Carefully, James J. Cramer

Jim Cramer's Real Money, James J. Cramer

How I Made $2,000,000 in the Stock Market, Nicolas Darvas

How to Become a Millionaire, Jim Slater & Tom Stevenson

How to Pick Stocks, Fred W. Frailey

How to Pick Stocks Like Warren Buffett, Timothy Vick

Investing Secrets of the Masters, Charles E. Babin & William J. Donovan

Investing With Anthony Bolton: The Anatomy of a Stock Market Phenomenon,
    Jonathan Davis

Magnet Investing (Second Edition), Jordon L. Kimmel

Million Dollar Portfolio, David Gardner & Tom Gardner

More Wealth Without Risk, Charles J. Givens

Multiple Streams of Income, Robert G. Allen

No Bull: My Life In and Out of the Market, Michael Steinhardt (An excellent
    autobiography)

Nothing Down, Robert G. Allen

One Up On Wall Street, Peter Lynch & John Rothchild

Rule #1, Phil Town

Secrets of the Millionaires, T. Harv Eker

Security Analysis Principles and Techniques, Benjamin Graham & David L.
    Dodd & Sidney Cottle
Start Late, Finish Rich, David Bach
Stocks for the Long Run, Jeremy J. Siegel
The Alternative Answer, Bob Rice
The Automatic Millionaire, David Bach
The Automatic Millionaire Homeowner, David Bach
The Best 100 Stocks to Own For Under $25 (Second Edition), GeneWalden
The Essential Buffett, Robert G. Hagstrom Jr.
The 5 Lessons a Millionaire Taught Me, Richard Paul Evans
The Forever Portfolio: How to Pick Stocks That You Can Hold for the Long Run,
    James Altucher
The Great 401(k) Hoax, William Wolman & Anne Colamosca
The Intelligent Investor, Benjamin Graham
The Jubak Picks, Jim Jubak
The Little Book of Main Street, Jonathan Clements
The Little Book That Beats the Market, Joel Greenblatt
The Mathematics of Investing, Michael C. Thomsett
The Money Coach's Guide to Your First Million, Lynnette Khalfani
The New Buffettology, Mary Buffett & David Clark
The 100 Best Stocks to Own In America (Sixth Edition), Gene Walden
The Richest Man Who Ever Lived, Steven K. Scott
The Street.Com, Dave Kansas
The Successful Investor, William J. O'Neil
The Warren Buffett Portfolio, Robert G. Hagstrom
The Warren Buffett Way, Robert G. Hagstrom
The Zulu Principle, Jim Slater
Warren Buffett and the Interpretation of Financial Statements, Mary Buffett &
    David Clark
Warren Buffett Invests Like a Girl, Louann Lofton
Wealth Without Risk, Charles J. Givens

Thank you for Reading!

Dear Reader,

It has been my intention to not waste your time with a bunch of useless information but to teach you the same powerful principles and strategies used by some of the world's most successful investment pros to build wealth. It is my greatest desire that you feel that I have succeeded in accomplishing both tasks.

For those of you that are new to investing, it is my hope that you have gained a newfound knowledge about investing that will save you a great sum of time and money and will put you on a path to building real wealth that will allow you to achieve the financial independence that you desire.

For the seasoned investor, it is my sincere hope that you have also found this book to contain some valuable information that will help you to become an even better investor by adding to the knowledge that you already possess about investing.

I have certainly enjoyed sharing with you the knowledge that I have obtained through more than ten years of research, study, and portfolio management. If you have enjoyed this book and have a minute to spare, I would really appreciate a short review on the page or website where you bought the book. Even if you didn't like it, I would enjoy your feedback. Reviews can be tough to come by these days, and you, the reader, has the power to make or break a book.

Thank you so much for reading *You Can Invest Like A Stock Market Pro*.

In gratitude,

James Pattersenn Jr.

James Pattersenn Jr.

INDEX

Symbols

10-Ks, 24-25
401(k), 16, 39, 70, 126, 187, 208
403(b), 16, 70

A

Abraham, 201
Accountant, 84
Accounting, 25, 84, 124, 145
Accounting skills, 25
Acquired, 125, 130, 167
Acquisition, 21, 130, 155, 167
Active, 60, 131-132
Actively manage, 5, 194
Actively managed, 26, 131, 178, 189, 191
Actively managed funds, 26
Aecom Technology Corp., 128
Aeropostale Inc., 78-80, 82, 85
aerospace, 149, 167
Aetna Inc., 125
Air Methods Corp., 167, 169, 171, 173
Airline industry, 60, 63-64
Al Neuharth, 3
alcohol, 201
alcohol abuse, 201
allegations, 168
Almost Family, 92-93, 145
Almost Family Inc, 92, 145
Amazon, 62, 176
Amazon.com, 62
America's Big Three, 187

American Airlines, 60
American families, 183
American Insurance Group, 187
Americans, 7, 28, 124
Ameritrade, 112, 197
Analysis, 25, 40, 81, 85, 90, 92, 102, 118, 140-141, 208
Analysts, 49, 91-94, 98-100, 106, 137-139, 141, 143, 146-147, 149-150, 154, 156-158, 166-168, 175-176
Analysts' estimates, 92, 149
Anika Therapeutics, 146-149, 152, 161, 174, 190
Anika Therapeutics Inc., 146-149, 152, 161, 174, 190
Annual cash flow statement, 83
Annual Earnings Growth Rate, 106
Annual fees, 19
Annual rate, 91, 93, 96, 106, 113, 123, 125, 128, 130, 134-136, 138-143, 145-147, 149-152, 154-155, 157-159, 161-174, 190
Annual reports, 24-25
Apple Inc., 157-158, 161, 164, 172
Appreciation, 140, 147, 178
Assets, 42, 81, 153, 155, 168
ATM cards, 19
Atwood Oceanics, 106-107, 137, 139, 142, 164, 174
Auto insurance, 18

Automatic transfers, 112
Automotive manufacturers, 187
Average annual P/E ratio, 97-100, 156
Average cost, 107, 126, 130-131, 135-141, 143-150, 152, 154, 160-161, 163, 166-167, 170-173, 198
Average Cost Per Share, 126, 130, 137-141, 143-146, 149, 154, 161, 167, 170-172, 198
Awesome, 79, 201

B

Baby Wal-Marts, 176
Balanced funds, 70
Bank, 11, 19, 62, 112, 168, 180, 186-187
Bank of America., 186
Banking, 19, 24, 62, 168, 183
Banking stocks, 62, 183
Bankruptcy, 60, 85, 185, 187
Bargain Stocks, 198
Bargains, 39, 41-42, 89
Base year, 78
Basic training, 12-13
Bear market, 186
Bear Stearns, 183, 186
Bed Bath & Beyond, 97-98, 176-178
Benjamin Graham, 8, 25, 40, 93, 95, 118, 199, 208
Berkshire Hathaway, 31, 33
Bernard Baruch, 30, 48
Bernard Kelly, 29, 207